INSTRUCTIONAL TELEVISION

Bold New Venture

ALREADY PUBLISHED IN THE

Bold New Venture *Series*

TEAM TEACHING
INDEPENDENT STUDY
FLEXIBLE SCHEDULING
NONGRADED SCHOOLS IN ACTION
TEACHING FOR CREATIVE ENDEAVOR
PROGRAMMED INSTRUCTION
EDUCATIONAL MANPOWER
INSTRUCTIONAL MEDIA CENTER
INSTRUCTIONAL TELEVISION

INSTRUCTIONAL TELEVISION

Bold New Venture

EDITED BY

RICHARD C. BURKE

INDIANA UNIVERSITY PRESS

BLOOMINGTON AND LONDON

Copyright © 1971 by Indiana University Press

ALL RIGHTS RESERVED

*No part of this book may be reproduced or utilized in any
form or by any means, electronic or mechanical, including
photocopying and recording, or by any information storage
and retrieval system, without permission in writing from
the publisher. The Association of American University
Presses Resolution on Permissions constitutes the only
exception to this prohibition.*

Published in Canada by Fitzhenry & Whiteside Limited,
Don Mills, Ontario

Library of Congress catalog card number: 70-143243
ISBN: 0-253-33018-1

Manufactured in the United States of America

Preface

Bold New Venture Series

Aᴍᴇʀɪᴄᴀɴ ᴇᴅᴜᴄᴀᴛɪᴏɴ is emerging as a new frontier. Staggering challenges brought about by the contemporary demand for quality education for a bulging and diverse student population must be met. Old solutions for new problems will not suffice.

Pioneer educators are testing promising new programs and practices to effect fundamental improvement in the schools. Healthy dissatisfactions have led to the belief that if the schools are to be significantly better, they will have to be substantially different. Both the substance and the form of instruction are undergoing searching reappraisal. Exciting innovations have been instituted in schools scattered throughout the country. The *Bold New Venture* series is designed to inform educators and the interested public about these new developments and to assist in their evaluation.

The books in the series differ from much of the professional literature in education. The contributors, for the most part, are practitioners. Admittedly they are partial to their topics. Nevertheless, pitfalls are exposed and candid treatment is given to the issues. Emphasis has been put on reporting *how* as well as *why* new practices and programs were inaugurated. The volumes in this series are intended to be a stimulus to the conversation which must take place if fresh methods of teaching are to find their way into the schools.

Topics included in the *Bold New Venture* series include team teaching, flexible scheduling, independent study, the nongraded school, instructional materials centers, data processing, small group instruction, and technological aids.

While journalists criticize, scholars theorize about, and philosophers analyze education, the teachers of America must act. Educators must leap from theory to practice in individualizing instruction. More responsibility must be given and accepted by youngsters for their own learning. Intellectual inquiry must become full-time, lei-sure-time, and life-time pursuits.

Progress in education does not always come by the process of ad-dition with more teachers, more books, more courses, and more money. Real improvement can come from original uses of scarce hu-man talent, precious time, and new methods.

Because it is intended primarily for teachers and administrators, the *Bold New Venture* series focuses on the practical problems of teaching. What has been operationally successful for some teachers may have application for other teachers. If new practices or pro-grams result from these books, then the series will have fulfilled its aim, for the *Bold New Venture* books are calls and guides to action.

Bloomington, Indiana   EDWARD G. BUFFIE

Contents

Introduction

Johnny brooke, eight years old, is a student in Iowa Public Education Concenter 417. To his parents' consternation, Johnny's "classes" at Concenter 417 apparently consist only of him.

The pupils frequently do gather in groups, for seminar-like discussions; for visits to museums, the zoo, the symphony, the supermarket, the monorail station; for physical education; for public speaking; for meetings of the Junior Astronauts Club Johnny belongs to; and for a variety of other activities. And rehearsals of his choral group seem to be conducted in much the same way as the school classrooms his grandmother described to him from her girlhood.

But for the most part the children meet with their teachers individually. In addition to the "regular" teachers, there are some rather unusual people on the instructional staff. Johnny's favorites last year were a concert violinist and a furniture designer, and his favorite this year is a retired sea captain. Johnny knows where Brazil is and what Sao Paulo looks like because he signaled his learning console to project films that would show him, but it was his conversations with the sea captain that moved Johnny to ask the console about Brazil in the first place.

The learning console at which Johnny spends much of his time in Concenter 417 appears to be an enclosed desk with a television set and a typewriter built into it. He starts his lesson by inserting his aluminum identification plate into the console demand-slot. Within a few seconds the screen projects a problem in mathematics. Johnny recognizes it; he had the same problem at the end of yesterday's lesson. He picks up his electronic stylus and writes the answer on his response slate; it resembles an old-fashioned square of blackboard except that it has several hundred thousand tiny pores that receive impulses from the stylus and translate handwriting to machine language.

A voice from the speaker in the console congratulates Johnny on getting the right answer, then urges, "Now try this one," as the screen projects a new problem. If he gets a wrong answer, the screen projects the same kind of problem a different way; if Johnny gets three wrong in a row, a soft tone rings in Betty Raschke's lapel alarm and brings her into his console.

Dr. Raschke, the concenter monitor, is not the only person

keeping track of Johnny's progress. His console and concenter—like all the other concenters around the Davenport metropolitan area, more numerous than neighborhood heliports—are connected to the Educational Resource Center downtown. There, the record of Johnny's progress that has been tabulated by computers is combed by a team of psychologists, programmers, expert teachers of everything from arithmetic to zoology, remedial specialists, and guidance counselors.

Neither Johnny nor anyone else knows what grade he is in. As quickly as he masters one "learning unit," his programmed courses offer more difficult material. He proceeds at his own pace, neither holding back other students on subjects he finds difficult nor being slowed down by them on subjects in which he excels.

Johnny rides to Concenter 417 each morning with his sister, Fran, who is nineteen and hopes to be a surgeon. She takes her course work in the morning, on a console one floor above Johnny's, and goes to a medical center in the afternoon for laboratory work.

The Brooke family has two learning consoles at home. Fran uses hers in the evening to ask the Educational Resource Center for help on her calculus or literature research papers. When her father is in an ambitious mood, he picks up the program guide and dials either Elementary Japanese Conversation or Advanced Econometrics. He has not yet decided whether to accept a promotion that would require moving to his firm's Kyoto branch, but if he does, he will be ready. Mrs. Brooke has decided, and three afternoons a week she dials Oriental Cuisine, and watches it on her kitchen extension screen.

In Johnny's world, education never stops; learning is a year-round, lifelong process.[1]

After reading the story of Johnny Brooke and Dr. Raschke, your reaction might be: "How much easier it must have been to teach in 1910! No one was asking any questions about education, and no one really paid too much attention to what went on in the schools. The teacher transmitted the heritage of the past to his students; he drilled them in their letters and numbers; and when they got big enough to go to work, they just stopped coming to school."

Since the innocent age of 1910 we have had two world wars, a depression, a Sputnik scare, an information explosion, a population explosion, a massive civil rights movement, and a revolution in science and technology. In the 1970's more people are demanding more education, and there is no doubt that the demands will continue to grow.

What we learned about physical science twenty years ago, or even ten years ago, is no longer adequate in dealing with the latest happenings in space travel, nor is our comparatively limited knowledge of biology sufficient to enable us to keep up with the latest discoveries in genetics and medical science. There is simply more material to be covered now than there was twenty years ago, and teachers are obligated to do the best they can to cover it. The United States Office of Education has calculated that there are now 65 to 70 million students enrolled in our schools, colleges, and universities. We have been told that there is a serious shortage of teachers which will become even more critical in the next ten years. Our present school buildings are overcrowded and those under construction are obsolete as soon as they are completed.

In looking for the solutions to all these problems, we often become rigid in our thinking. We talk about teacher-student ratio, school space, and curriculum units as if they were terms of an inflexible equation. Let me illustrate what I mean with an excerpt from a speech by John Goodlad, Dean of the Graduate School of Education at the University of California, Los Angeles:

> More than a year ago, a creative, imaginative school superintendent in California came to visit me. He was excited, as he should have been, about his notion of creating a true laboratory school in the public school setting. He wanted to begin with none of the old assumptions; to start from the very beginning. After he had talked a while and I was sharing his enthusiasm, I began to ask some specific questions.
>
> "When was the school to open?" "More than a year hence." "Had anything been done about employing teachers?" "Yes, a principal had been selected and employment was proceeding." "How many teachers were to be employed?"
>
> The answer worked out to a figure of one teacher for every twenty-eight pupils, or approximately twenty teachers. I asked, "Why twenty. Why not five, or seven, or ten?" My visitor became a little irritated. I pushed on. "How large is the school to be?" The answer indicated that there were to be rooms or open, flexible spaces for nearly six hundred pupils. I then asked why the school was not being designed for half this number. Now my visitor was very irritated. He thought I was playing a sadistic game.
>
> Of course I was not. The point I was making is that we effect our major decisions by tradition before getting to the few things we change. We assume that there will be X number of qualified teachers for Y number of children. And we assume that we will construct a school building large enough for all of the children to be housed. But there is no reason at all why we could not em-

ploy half the usual quota of fully qualified teachers, using the balance of our money for part-time specialists and a host of instructional aids. And there is no reason at all why we could not plan an educational program that required only half a school building, with the balance of the money going to trips, special projects, and individualized activities supervised by the staff or even programmed by a computer.[2]

What I think Goodlad is suggesting is that we have to look at the business of teaching and learning without any preformed ideas as to what is "normal" or "accepted practice." Through team teaching, flexible scheduling, the nongraded school, independent study, and instructional technology we are beginning to realize that the best system for teaching and learning is one which guarantees maximum freedom and flexibility to teacher, student, and administrator.

Television

This book is about one aspect of technology in education—television. When television was first introduced into our schools some educators felt that they were witnessing the beginning of a new era in American education. They saw television as the solution to all of their problems: Television would relieve the teacher shortage by making one good teacher available to an unlimited number of students; the quality of instruction would be upgraded because the television teacher could present material of higher quality in less time than it took the classroom teacher; television would give every child a front row seat for demonstrations, experiments and language instruction; television was, in short, the greatest invention since the printed book. There are studies, annual reports, feature articles on Hagerstown, Maryland; the state-wide systems of South Carolina, Alabama, and Georgia; the Chicago TV junior college; and dozens of others. These are the success stories in the literature of instructional television.

At the same time, there were teachers and administrators who looked on television as just another intrusive gadget in the classroom. It interfered with the true business of education by disturbing the delicate relationship between teacher and student. Television was threatening to invade their classrooms and they wanted nothing to do with this purveyor of cartoons and commercials.

There are not as many stories about the failure of instructional television, but obviously there have been instances where television failed to contribute anything to a particular learning situation. Where television has proven unsatisfactory, we are likely to be told any number of things: It was too expensive; program quality was poor; teachers were not interested in it; students could not learn from it; parents did not want it in the schools; too much trouble with the television receivers—in short, it did not work out, and a lot of time and money had been wasted.

No one could say with absolute certainty why some educators accepted television, while others rejected it. Perhaps enthusiasm, sincere desire for improvement, and willingness to change would account partly for the positive point of view, and fear, uncertainty, and resistance to change would account partly for the negative point of view.

There are, of course, people who still see television as the all-purpose educational tool, and there are those who still refuse to have anything to do with it. In recent years, however, most educators have adopted a more reasonable and balanced point of view toward instructional television (or for that matter any form of instructional technology) than the two extremes I have been describing. What is happening now is that we are shifting our emphasis from television to instruction. This shift in emphasis is extremely important, because it forces us to ask some basic questions about teaching and learning. We want to know more about how people learn and how we can encourage and facilitate the process. We are now thinking about education using a modified systems approach: What goes into the process; what do we do in the various stages of the process; and what do we want as the finished product? What in fact is education all about?

We hope to provide in this book some basic information about instructional television to educators who are concerned with the problems of teaching and learning. We do not claim that television has any magic properties, merely that it could make a valuable contribution to the process of education, and it is therefore worthy of consideration.

INSTRUCTIONAL TELEVISION

TELEVISION

Bold New Venture

CHAPTER 1

The Role of Television in Education

by

Lewis A. Rhodes

WHAT IS THERE ABOUT TELEVISION that makes it an exciting and powerful tool in the process of education? How does television relate to the problems of learning, teaching, and school management? Probably in the past few years too much has been claimed for television, and in all fairness it must be said that as an instructional device it has certain strengths as well as certain limitations. But if we remember that television is a medium of communication and not only an electronic teaching device, we are less likely to make exaggerated claims on its behalf. Let us take a look at some basic characteristics of television.

Live television coverage of a special session of the United Nations, a space shot from Cape Kennedy, or any special event "live via satellite" creates a sense of immediacy, a "you are there" feeling. Television has the characteristic of "nowness"—a sense of involvement in the present.

All communication is basically person-to-person, but the means of

3

distributing it may be mass created. Television, possibly because of its immediacy, can help create a one-to-one line of communication. A communicator can maintain eye contact and mind contact with the intended receiver of his communication.

With television we can move ideas, people, and resources from place to place, thereby multiplying their effectiveness and value. The outstanding teacher is no longer confined to teaching relatively few students in a lifetime. The resources of our great museums, art galleries, and libraries can be made available to institutions and individuals separated by space and frequently by time.

Because the image on the television screen can be structured and controlled, the viewer can be shown only what should be at the focus of attention at any given moment. This focusing of attention tends to eliminate a great deal of distraction and helps to maintain the one-to-one line of communication.

Applying Television to the Problems of Education

Imagine a traveler of the mid-twentieth century who has never heard about the invention of the airplane. In planning a trip, his goals and objectives would obviously be limited by the capabilities of the "hardware" (trains, buses, and automobiles) of which he is aware. Like the traveler with no knowledge of airplanes, education has been limited to those goals that seem realistically attainable. While striving for individual learning opportunities we have had to settle for group teaching; we acknowledge the need for equal educational opportunities but we have had to accept the restraints of geography as well as social and economic conditions; we realize the need for relevant, developmental curriculum materials, but we have had to accept mass-produced, standardized resources.

It has been difficult at times to realize that we can actually achieve many of our educational goals today. Quite often we have the necessary technology, but we do not always see the relationship between long-hoped-for educational goals and unfamiliar technologies. It may be easier to understand this relationship by looking at the nature of some of our most familiar educational problems. Most of these goal-impeding problems relate to the organization, distribution, storage, and sharing of information, ideas, and personnel.

Organizing Information

If you were asked to present in five or ten minutes a talk or a lesson that ordinarily takes thirty minutes, what would you do? No doubt you would soon realize that the key to presenting more information in less time is organization. With two or three hours of preparation it is entirely possible that the ten-minute presentation can be as effective as the thirty-minute one.

Because of the great amount of information that has to be communicated to children in our schools, the role of the teacher has evolved to that of presenter of information during eighty to ninety percent of the time he teaches. It becomes more obvious as one looks higher in the grades; in high school and in college, teaching and telling become practically synonymous. Moreover, the knowledge explosion and methodological reform movement is pushing subject-matter information lower into the grades, e.g., science, foreign languages, and advanced mathematics. The problem of finding the time for the teacher to spend in guiding and motivating the individual student is becoming a critical one in the elementary grades as well.

If we can increase presentation quality, while decreasing the amount of time spent in actual presentation by providing more time for effective organization of a lesson, a rationale for a cooperative arrangement begins to take form. If one teacher could be given the time and appropriate assistance to prepare, organize, and present the lesson, the time saved on the presentation of information alone could be returned to the classroom teacher to spend on the more important, but frequently impossible, functions of guiding individual learning. Television provides a means of bringing a complementary, well-organized presentation into the classroom, while giving the classroom teacher more time for the creative teaching aspects of stimulating, motivating, and developing the learning activities that involve the student, with the information that was presented. The television lesson serves, in this case, as a complement to the classroom teacher, rather than a time-adding supplement.

Within the presentation itself, the television teacher can structure the information in such a way as to stimulate the response he desires in the viewing student. The person presenting material on television can make use of a variety of other media such as slides, films, and photographs to focus the attention of the viewer on only that which should be seen. With video-tape recording, the lesson can be shown to a representative sample of the intended audience before widespread use. Those elements of the lesson that fail to attain their intended objectives can be retaped if necessary. This latter aspect is particularly important when television lessons are being developed with behavioral or performance objectives in mind.

Distribution of Information

A great many of the problems of education involve the movement of people to information or information to people. Today's problems of geographic and cultural deprivation both in rural areas and in cities are due to some extent to the inaccessibility of resources. Historically we know that education has suffered from limited resources—material and human. Effective tactics for dealing with the problem have been limited primarily to the highway and the hallway. On the highway, first the circuit-riding teachers went to the students, then the school bus moved students to central collections of teachers, and most recently the mobile demonstration units, bookmobiles, etc., move resources again to the students. The hallway, meanwhile, has provided a route for the student to get to the central information storage devices—the library and the subject-matter specialist teacher.

While education continues to resort to the wheel to deal with its distribution problems, television could be providing the electronic hallways and highways which make possible the movement of the inspired thought, the limited resource, or the specialist in short supply on a more frequent basis. Few states have used television to deal effectively with the problems of geographic deprivation on a systematic basis, though several already have the hardware or distribution capability to do so.

In its distributive function, television can allow schools to deal not only with the obvious information movement problems of instruction, but also with the equally severe problems in administrative and supervisory communication; for instance, as educational systems get larger, ineffective two-way communication results in the depersonalization of the administration. Staffs become too large to meet in any one place, and faculties, in increasing numbers, have had to organize to make their voices heard. Some school systems have been able to make use of television to disseminate policy decisions and other information on current school matters on a continuing basis. It has even been possible to build a feedback capability for questions into the system through use of ordinary telephones.

With teacher shortages and the resultant mobility of staff there are often severe problems of orientation to the school systems' procedures. Several school systems have used television to provide opportunities for observing particular classroom procedures and instruction in other aspects of the school system. The increase in man's knowledge coupled with the changing methodologies for dealing with this knowledge has made it increasingly difficult for teachers to remain up to date. Several school systems have used television to provide in-service resources on a systematic basis to upgrade both the information and the methodologies of the professional and administrative staffs.

It is increasingly apparent that these administrative and supervisory communication problems can all be dealt with effectively through electronic media that make possible immediate personal communication, distribution of the most current ideas, and nondisruptive observation of behavior models. Television, by providing the simultaneous communication links between the elements of the collection of buildings that we now call a school system, can make possible the relationships that are the primary structure of an organic, interactive institution.

Managing Time and Preserving Information

Television has always been a tool to bridge space, but since the advent of recording devices, application has been made to those problems that require, in addition, the bridging of time. The most obvious applications have been the storage of the nonreplicable incident and the observation of behavior. In the latter case, individuals have always had to depend on others for evaluation of their own behavior, whether involved in athletics, demonstration teaching, or other professional skills training. Today, through the utilization of the video-tape recorder with its "instant replay" characteristic, individuals may immediately analyze and critique their own activities.

At many schools the combination of a small video-tape recorder and a portable camera has been built into an effective system called Micro-teaching which permits a student teacher to learn specific teaching behavioral skills through a teach-critique-reteach process. Outside of formal education, business and industry have been creatively applying this technique to the development of sales and administrative skills in their employees, with many reports of significant reductions in training times.

With television as a research tool, the behavioral scientist can capture behavior much as the biologist encases a specimen and takes it back to the laboratory for study. The recording may be edited to expand or shrink time or to show cause and effect; and time can be run forward, backward, or even frozen. Teacher education libraries can store examples of good and poor teaching behavior, edited and condensed to provide experiences beyond the capability of on-the-spot classroom viewing.

Role and Responsibility

Two definitions are given for a medium: "a substance through which a force acts or an effect is transmitted" and "that through which or by which anything is accomplished." Another way of saying it would be to construct a model in which we have the elements of stimulus, medium, and response. Looking at the model from one point of view we could say that the "medium carries the stimulus"; from the other point of view, we could say that "the medium makes possible the creation of the desired response." The medium does not change—only our perception or point of view of it changes. So far in education, our perception of television's role has been limited too much by the view that television in itself is a stimulus, rather than something through which we accomplish other important things related to our basic objectives. We have thus neglected the important fact that the medium has logistic attributes which can be utilized in the management of educational resources.

As a management tool one of television's chief values is that it can permit the establishment of *new* relationships among the human resources of an educational system, thereby multiplying their value and effectiveness. Television can make it possible for a school to implement new patterns of staff utilization, such as team teaching, disseminate new or locally developed curricula system-wide, and provide the stimulus for more flexible schemes of classroom organization. In the full context of humanistic education this role promises unlimited opportunities.

As with any tool, a fundamental familiarity with television is a prerequisite to an understanding of its application to the problems with which we are most familiar. Education's present decision-makers, having grown up without the technologies now available, cannot easily make this application. Television, therefore, has not been seen as a tool of the operating educator as much as it has been considered the province of the broadcaster, the media specialist, or the technologist. Television cannot fulfill a functional role in education until it is understood and applied by those who have both the general responsibility for setting the objectives of education, and the direct responsibility for dealing with the problems that hinder the attainment of these objectives.

CHAPTER 2

Television at the Elementary Level

by
PAULINE HADD

THE ELEMENTARY SCHOOL TEACHER is a jack-of-all-trades and surprisingly enough master of many of them. The list of his duties is a staggering one, and it has been said that "the elementary school teacher needs the stamina of a mule and the arms of an octopus." Many elementary teachers spend all day with one class, often instructing the students in all subjects, some of which the teacher may not be interested in or not even particularly suited to teach. Some help has come in the form of television.

For the classroom teacher television is a reality; it came whether he was ready for it or not. Teachers who have not used television in their classes tend to be suspicious of it and to resist its use. This resistance by elementary teachers does not persist, however, and they soon learn to depend on television as a teaching resource. Niccolò Machiavelli wrote in *The Prince,* "Where the willingness is great, the difficulties cannot be great." I found the willingness, and as I gain more experience with the proper uses of television, my appreciation of its value increases.

Using Television—A Cooperative Venture

The TV set will never replace the classroom teacher, but as an elementary teacher I am not a specialist, and I welcome help from the television teacher. Teaching with the use of TV is a cooperative venture, or it may be looked on as team teaching, especially in the case of closed-circuit television.

The TV teacher is a partner in my classroom. Every Tuesday afternoon he takes over part of my teaching assignment. He presents, explains, and demonstrates major points in the lesson and stimulates student interest. My job is to clear up misunderstandings, make assignments, evaluate the students, and provide for group and individual activity. The success or failure of the TV teacher's efforts will depend heavily on my performance as a classroom teacher. He may do a superb job, but it will count for little if I fail in my half of the task. We must work as a team and support each other's efforts.

Teachers make use of television in a variety of ways but TV lessons are never complete without help from the classroom teacher. The director of elementary education in a South Dakota city said, "In my opinion, the teacher who uses television to the best advantage uses her teacher's manual very carefully. The teachers who are most effective use a great deal of supplementary material to motivate and to add to the substance of the TV presentation. As in any teaching, those who effectively stimulate class discussions do a splendid job in making television meaningful to their students." A teacher in the lower elementary grades commented, "The presentation on television seems to be an introduction and a preliminary view of the material to be learned. The in-depth teaching and additional reference and supplementary work, then, becomes the responsibility of the classroom teacher." Another teacher reported, "For the student in primary grades it is a branching out into the world of experience and new personalities. Follow-up activities broaden into many areas of classroom study."

One sixth grade teacher utilizes television in her science course by introducing the topic of the week's lesson with the necessary vocabulary at the beginning of the week. The pupils then make up a list of research questions and projects that they would like to work on during the week, as individuals or in groups. Each week the groups are varied so that all have the opportunity and the experience of working with different members of the class. One or two periods are spent working on research or projects to be presented to the class in the last period or period and a half. Sometimes the teacher gives a specific reading assignment in one of the multitexts to provide further background before individual research. By Friday the class has a basic understanding of the material to be covered on TV and the lesson helps to clarify their concepts and ideas. Sometimes it brings up new questions to work on the next week.

Some of the specific things I do in utilizing television in fifth grade science can easily be adapted to other subject areas on almost any grade level. Each pupil has a notebook just for science that is used as a permanent place for important notes and key words as we develop a unit of work. We are constantly gathering information from many sources since we do not have the traditional single basic text. Some teachers have their pupils fill in a blank outline during the telecast. For some students, outlining or note-taking may encourage concentration, but for others, it may be a distraction that causes them to miss important points of the lesson. I prefer that the televised program have the undivided attention of all students; therefore, they listen with cleared desks.

I prepare my class for the program on an earlier day. Younger children will need a short refresher preparation just before the viewing and a short follow-up session afterwards. In my fifth grade class I use the chalkboard or the overhead projector to present the key words and some of the ideas to watch for in the program. Occasionally I have a ditto copy of the key terms prepared for each child. I try to vary my introduction to each week's lesson. The TV teacher repeats the words and their meanings; however, repetition is often useful and necessary in the learning process.

If I have seen the lesson before, I prepare the children for specific references in the program. I watch out for local references in TV series developed elsewhere. When our TV teacher took us to the James River, my class knew that it was not the James River near our town in South Dakota but the James River in Virginia. We related this fact to our earlier study of the settling of the eastern part of our country. When a TV teacher told my class that there are about as many bees in a beehive as there are people in Lowell it had little meaning for them. With the help of reference books we found a town near us whose population would compare to the number of bees in a hive. A research question in a TV manual referred to the native plants and animals in Boston Common; I simply substituted the name of our local park. If a teacher is not disturbed by a few local references in a series, the pupils will not mind either.

The Telecast

I check the tuning of the TV set before my class comes to the room after the lunch hour. About two minutes before our program begins I turn on the TV set but keep the volume off. The children take this as a signal to clear their desks and those who sit up front too close to the TV set move to the back of the room. Each child places his chair in a position so that he can view the lesson in comfort. I adjust the volume and I am ready to sit in the back of the room with my TV teacher's manual and my own notebook and pen. I do more than just sit and enjoy the program. If it is the first time I have viewed the program, I am very busy taking notes; if I have seen it before, I make the notes I already have more complete. I jot down ideas for the unit; I watch the children to see what their reactions are; and I am alert for points which need to be discussed later. During one recent telecast David raised his hand and then glanced back at me a bit foolishly because he had been lost in his thoughts and had forgotten momentarily that the TV teacher could not see his hand. I made a note to ask him later what he had wanted to say.

Repetition is helpful to the learning process. Often the TV teacher strengthens and emphasizes what I have been teaching. I have seen the pleased and understanding looks on my pupils' faces as our TV teacher explains or demonstrates something which they have already done. They turn quietly to our bulletin board and look with satisfaction at Kay's drawings of high and low pressure systems, Chris's chart of the planetary winds, or Debra's and Rick's diagrams explaining land and sea breezes. When the TV teacher explains and shows us different kinds of hygrometers and ends by saying that there are still other kinds, there on our bulletin board is Elizabeth's hygrometer which she made by using paper and a solution of cobalt chloride.

It is usually best to allow the program to proceed without interruption from the teacher. My follow-up period the day of the telecast is usually rather short. By the time my fifth graders have seen a thirty-minute program they are not eager to spend much time in a follow-up. Except for taking care of urgent questions and points, it is better to wait until the following day when there is ample time to do justice to the follow-up.

Anticipated Problems

Most of the problems that I had anticipated in the use of television were solved without too much trouble. My school had enough basic textbooks and reference books so that I could teach easily without following any one book closely. Parents and relatives buy many good up-to-date reference books for children, and the children, in turn, enjoy sharing these tools with their classmates. There has never been a lack of books to use in conjunction with television in my classroom.

In my first year of using television it was necessary to reorganize my science file. It was an added burden, but I would have had to do it if a new textbook had been introduced in the course instead of a new television series of programs. It appeared in the beginning that there would be no time to teach health with thirty television science programs to be shown and taught during the school year. I taught some health units in the fall before the television series began and some additional units in the spring after the series was over. Some TV science lessons do not require or justify spending a full week on them, and I can work in two days or more of health instruction. A teacher should be allowed to use her own judgment in deciding how much time must be allotted to the introduction and follow-up of each program. School time is too precious to waste and no program intended for widespread general use should require the same amount of time for all who view it.

I wanted my student teacher from a nearby university to have as many teaching experiences as possible while she was with me. She was assigned to my classroom mornings only, but she viewed the television lesson in the afternoon during her student teaching laboratory period at the university at the same time as my fifth graders watched in the classroom. I conducted the immediate follow-up period, and my student teacher conducted the extended follow-up period the next morning during science class.

Evaluation of Televised Lessons by Teachers and Pupils

The classroom teacher is often called on to evaluate a TV lesson or unit of lessons. He can be a better judge if he fully understands the purposes of the lesson or unit. He should provide constructive criticism and follow it with ways in which the presentation might be improved. The more specific the classroom teacher can be, the greater the value of the criticism to the studio teacher. Fairness is essential; if an excellent job was done for most of the lesson, the studio teacher should not be made to feel that the entire lesson was a waste of time. A joint evaluation by several teachers who have used the same telecast tends to be most valuable.

Some schools occasionally have students answer evaluating questionnaires immediately after viewing a lesson. These should not be used in the lower elementary grades. The classroom teacher presenting the questionnaires to the students must be as objective as possible, because pupils tend to reflect his attitude toward lessons or even whole subject areas taught. At the end of a series of units taught with television, I asked my pupils to rate the units in order of their preference, using a secret ballot. I was not too surprised to find their results coinciding exactly with my personal feelings, though I had tried very hard to conceal them. The teacher's attitude is contagious in the classroom, and therefore he must always approach the lesson or series with a positive and objective attitude.

Pupils' Reactions to Use of Television

Various research projects support the theory that children learn as much or more when television is utilized. Research by Wilbur Schramm points out that elementary school children *think* they learn more from televised instruction than through traditional means. They believe this is so, more than high school and college students do. My fifth graders were asked to give their reaction to the use of the televised instruction series "Adventures in Science" produced by the Richmond, Virginia, Public Schools at WCVE–TV, with A. Edward Ooghe as the TV teacher. Some of their comments expressed in their own words appear below; the comments in parentheses are mine.

Kristel: "TV Science makes me want to do some research. It tells enough about it to get me interested but it does not tell all about it." (Kristel is a very capable worker who likes to find out things for herself.)

Julie: "The television and school are about the same." (I agree; I maintain that TV is just another teaching tool. When the TV set is wheeled into the classroom it should cause no more excitement or commotion than a projector or any other equipment we use in our school.)

Melanie: "TV is good because they give examples that we wouldn't see otherwise. It saves the classroom teacher time. The television explains things so that we can understand it better. The questions are fun to find out." (We saw step-by-step TV demonstrations involving very tiny and very intricate objects. Every student in the room had a front row seat. Time was saved for me.)

Teresa: "I like TV because it is interesting. I don't like it because it won't repeat things and I can't ask it questions." (And she loves to ask questions! She is the type who is constantly worrying about things and likes to be reassured by hearing something over and over again.)

Jim: "Sometimes if I don't understand something on TV, I can't raise my hand and ask him but I can always ask you. I always like to know what he says about things and compare it with what you say. (Sometimes the children forget their questions by the time the program is over. The children either consciously or unconsciously compare the teachings of the classroom and TV teachers. One child was astonished that the television teacher and I had used almost the same words to explain the meaning of a key word. It was no coincidence; I had used my teacher's manual.)

Richard: "The person on TV can do better experiments because he can get better materials." (The TV teacher can use materials which would be too costly, too rare, or too dangerous to be brought to or shown in my classroom.)

Andy: "I think about the only problem with school TV is that the TV teacher doesn't know if you've answered right or wrong, and so why have school TV if your regular teacher has to sit with you and watch it? On the other hand, it is fun to watch TV." (The TV teacher does not know if the pupils answer correctly, but I know. The TV teacher often asks a question and allows time for the pupils to answer orally before he supplies the correct answer. Occasionally a short-answer quiz is given by the TV teacher and Andy knows that I record the scores.)

David: "I think Mr. Ooghe's show is very good. I know it is easier for you." (How little he knows how much time I have spent preparing myself and them for the TV program and the follow-up which is to come! However, I am glad he thinks it is easier.)

Jean: "I think it is fun to look up questions that you give us that go with what Mr. Ooghe teaches and on what we should know." (In addition to the research questions presented by the TV teacher during the TV lesson, there were some suggested in the teacher's manual to use in the preparation of the following lesson. I could not get along without my manual. I am constantly trying to improve it and adjust it to my classes. A teacher should never ignore the manual.)

Jeff: "I like it because he explains everything clearly. He also gives us questions to answer the next time. It gives me ideas for doing new things." (During the TV lessons Mr. Ooghe often said, "I leave this for your investigation," or, "I'd like to pose a question." Sometimes he offered a partial explanation of a problem and then said, "I hope you will do additional research.")

Carol: "I like Mr. Ooghe because he explains big words and he doesn't rush through things." (Mr. Ooghe not only explained big words, he spelled them, wrote them on the chalkboard, and pronounced them. He sometimes used a word and its meaning in the same sentence; for example, "The flask is inverted or turned upside down.")

The children's remarks indicate that they think of our teacher as a real person. To help them feel closer to the television teacher I have told them a little about his life and his family. My students take pride in the fact that he became a television teacher because he auditioned for the job and was chosen. He is no stranger to us; when our class secretary wrote him a letter he answered the questions about which my class had wondered.

Strong Points of Television

Television makes available high quality teaching skills and resource people, and presents many areas of instruction that the classroom teacher is not prepared to handle. It is an unlimited source of visual aids, such as specimens, collections, photographs, and materials of various kinds, that are often unavailable to the elementary classroom teacher. For instance, via television, the class saw two different kinds of generators producing static electricity, visited a shipyard to watch a ship being loaded with scrap iron by a huge electromagnet, and observed a demonstration with a bimetal strip which explained perfectly how the metallic thermometer really worked. (One of the pupils had brought one to school to show as a "different kind of thermometer.")

My science classes have watched a cecropia moth emerge from its cocoon, a process which actually takes a half hour or more. By speeding it up on TV we saw the complete process, and there was no crowding around a table waiting for turns to look. In the same manner, we saw a daffodil open, wither, and die without waiting for days to observe each stage. In a study of food from the sea, we were taken on a commercial fishing trip via our TV screen. We learned about herring fishing, shrimp fishing, using oyster tongs, kinds of fishing nets, and preservation of fresh fish at sea. Such a fishing trip is far removed from my midwestern classroom but we learned much from it, including a good lesson in conservation.

The TV lesson on circulatory systems of various animals showed the beating hearts of a clam and a fish, and traced the circulation of blood in the tail fin of a fish. Again, all pupils could see equally well at the same time. The class saw close-up views of beavers' lodges when we studied animal homes. In the study of animal hibernation we observed the measurement of the temperature and heartbeat of a ground squirrel. This demonstration explained more fully why the salamander in our classroom vivarium was so sluggish and awkward when he occasionally poked his head from under the water dish where he had hibernated during the winter.

When studying animal sounds my pupils saw the actual vibration of vocal cords. They heard a song sparrow, and the sounds of howling monkeys which were taped by a graduate student doing research in Central America. With an expert as a guide they visited an entomology laboratory to study insects. Movies shown during a TV lesson of bats catching fruit flies in their mouths or tail membranes were part of a university research project.

Television can and does suggest a variety of related research problems. Classroom teachers get from television new and different approaches to subjects. It stimulates thinking and adds variety to the daily schedule. Television has appropriate settings and background enrichment which establishes atmosphere. The use of television can establish numerous possibilities for group or individual creative work.

One teacher pointed out, "The fact that the programs appeared on our local television stations also helped to inform the public of our broader and expanded science program." In one South Dakota town the "new math" series intended for lower elementary grades created so much interest among the parents viewing it at home that they organized a night class in order to keep in step with what their children were learning via television at school.

Many classroom teachers have commented on the time which is saved by TV demonstrations for science. The classroom teacher does not have to assemble the equipment, practice the demonstration, or clean the equipment.

Criticisms of Television in the Classroom

One teacher complained that "Experiments always work on TV. It frustrates my children when experiments don't always turn out right for them when they try the ones suggested on TV." I suspect the teacher was the frustrated one. An experiment at my school did not turn out as my co-worker and her class had hoped. They tried to hatch chicken eggs using a new incubator for the first time. Not one egg hatched. My co-worker, however, had a positive attitude toward experiments. She said, "I think we have some things to learn from our experience. Did we keep the incubator too moist? Did the thermometer give an accurate reading of the temperature? Can we tell by opening the eggs whether some of the eggs were too close to the light bulb? Were the eggs really fertilized ones?"

Television in the classroom makes the daily schedule more rigid than ever before. The problems involved in planning a classroom schedule around the teachers of art, music, reading improvement programs, speech therapy, band lessons, television programs, library and physical education periods, and recess grow worse each year.

Many teachers have expressed a preference for having motion pictures related to the units they are teaching instead of regularly scheduled television programs. Few school systems can afford to buy that many films and often when a teacher tries to rent a film relating to a unit, the film is unavailable at that particular time because another school has rented it.

It has been said by some teachers that at times the information is presented too rapidly for the children to comprehend. The slow achiever especially may have problems. This complaint reinforces the importance of the classroom teacher's role in bringing about understanding of the concepts and adapting the TV lesson to all pupils, just as he has to do with the textbooks.

Black and white television is a handicap at times when color is an essential part of the presentation; for example, testing for acids, bases, and salts in science when the change of color is an important factor. Has the time come for the introduction of color television in our schools just as we have it in many of our homes?

Some classroom teachers feel handicapped in not having sufficient materials available to supplement the television instruction. Textbooks seldom follow the material presented on TV. School systems should choose the following year's programs for each grade in time for the teachers to know what supplies and reference books need to be ordered to go along with the TV programs. In some school systems, supply orders are placed during the early spring for the fall session of school.

Physical Arrangements

The ideal way to view a TV lesson is in the regular classrooms with the children seated at their own desks. Sufficient TV sets should be provided to make it possible. At a school where the TV set was located in the library, the teacher felt that there were too many interruptions. Some schools have a TV set in the gymnasium and the children sit on the floor to view the lesson. This arrangement encourages wiggling, whispering, and lack of attention to the TV lesson, and there are always interruptions by people passing through.

Viewing should take place in the regular classroom in order that there be full realization that this is a class and not an entertainment program. One teacher observed that the attitude of a class brought in from another room was not as good as that of the students remaining in their own room. However, the visitors did not have as good previewing preparation as those who viewed the program in their own room.

It is important to consider the placement of what is commonly referred to as the "rear controls," which include vertical lines, horizontal hold, and height and width of the picture on the screen. If these rear controls are located at the top of the TV set and the set is on a high cart, it is virtually impossible for the teacher to operate the controls and see the screen at the same time, even when she risks life and limb to climb on a chair to reach the controls. Control knobs should be clearly marked and simplified instructions on tuning should be attached to each TV set. The Kirksville Public School System in Missouri has set a good example in providing the classroom teacher with simplified and clear tuning directions.

Another big problem has been the mechanical one that is involved in using any machine as a visual aid. Sometimes the TV set simply does not function properly, and there is a whole class sitting and watching. It is embarrassing not to be able to produce the program for them, and more important, they are missing the program for which they were prepared.

It is basic to the success of television in a school system to have the full support and favorable attitude of the top administrators. The principal and the various supervisors in each building using television must be completely familiar with the programs and their purposes. Principals and building supervisors should help the classroom teachers work out a schedule for the use of the television sets. For example, at the conclusion of the TV lesson in my room, I immediately wheel the TV set into the sixth grade room next door, since their program follows ours in just a few minutes. The administrators should also keep the classroom teachers well informed on changes in program and class schedules. Teachers get discouraged when they have prepared a class to view a program only to find it will not be shown.

Administrators and teachers must work together to coordinate the television programs with existing curricula. When television was first introduced into the fifth and sixth grades in my school, we had to restructure the science curriculum for all sciences which were not dealt with adequately in our television series. One teacher commented that if the television program is to be used as enrichment only, it probably will not be scheduled at the most opportune time; and if it is used as part of a curriculum, then the material planned as the curriculum for the particular grade is not taught. Each school system must decide how best to integrate TV into the school's curriculum, making whatever adjustments are necessary.

Many administrators like the idea of television in their school systems, but they have not made the needed effort to make full utilization possible. If adequate planning and attention are lacking, television may be too complicated and too cumbersome for the classroom teacher to use it. For television to be fully utilized, it must be efficient as well as effective.

It has been said of television that it is the most important new educational tool since the invention of movable type, which made possible the textbook. This new tool can be used correctly or it can be misused. Much good teaching is being done by utilizing television in our elementary schools today, because its proper and profitable use is underwritten by dedicated teachers.

CHAPTER 3

Television in the Secondary School

by
WANDA B. MITCHELL

There is a tide in the affairs of men
Which, taken at the flood, leads on to fortune;
Omitted, all the voyage of their life
Is bound in shallows and in miseries.
On such a full sea are we now afloat,
And we must take the current when it serves,
Or lose our ventures.
　　　　　　　—Shakespeare, *Julius Caesar*, IV,3

THAT WE ARE NOW AFLOAT on a full sea of educational television is obvious to anyone who critically examines the evidence. The 1971 Directory of the National Association of Educational Broadcasters listed more than 207 educational television stations on the air, and 16 additional licensees ready to begin operations within the year.[1] It has been estimated that about one-fifth of the nation's students have been exposed to instructional television.

In spite of this flood of television, the secondary schools lag behind the other levels of institutional education in the use of this potentially powerful medium. In January 1966 Dr. Lloyd Trump, executive secretary of the National Association of Secondary School Principals reported from a survey of 16,082 high school principals that only one out of five high schools was using television in any way and twenty-one percent of the users were in the Northeast. The attitude of high school principals was indicated by their responses to this question: Do you think technological advances, such as television, hold promise?[2]

15%	Yes, considerable
51%	Yes, some
15%	No, little, if any
1%	No, harmful
14%	Undecided

The reluctance of the secondary schools to use television more extensively is contrary to the enthusiastic endorsement of parents and other citizens expressed in the opinion survey made for the Charles F. Kettering Foundation (which awarded a grant of $1,200,000 for a project to get ideas out of research libraries and into the schools). This poll of parental opinion revealed that "the U. S. public is far ahead of present-day educators in their willingness to accept innovation in the schools. . . ."[3] Further indication of general public interest in television programs of an educational nature is the high audience rating received by the drivers test, the citizenship test, and the health tests televised by commercial networks.

Why, then, are the secondary schools using television less than the elementary and college levels? What are the characteristics, inherent in the secondary school organization, that seem to work against any general adoption of televised instruction at the high school level?

Problems

SCHEDULE

One of the most frequently mentioned problems in secondary school use of television is the difficulty of correlating broadcast time with the variety of high school bell schedules. The elementary school teacher in a self-contained classroom can switch language arts and science in order to view a science telecast at 10:15. The problem is less easily solved in high school where science classes may meet at 9:00, 10:30, 1:00, and 2:15, and the science telecast is from 9:30 to 10:00. Even in a single school district it would be unlikely that an American history lesson could be telecast at a time convenient for the juniors in all the high schools of the district.

Solution. The schedule problem is not unsolvable. Since the advent of video-tape recorders in the lower-price brackets, individual schools can record lessons for playback at a more convenient time. Educational stations can repeat a lesson at different times on several days if their schedule is not too crowded.

The number of schools now operating on modular, flexible schedules and using the "no bells ring" pattern suggests that scheduling in the use of television will no longer be a problem.

CURRICULUM CONTENT

Another complaint by secondary schools reluctant to use television is that the content of the television lesson is not appropriate to their curriculum. High schools restricted by state or district courses of study find that a television series presents the right material at the wrong time in the semester or emphasizes the one unit which the classroom teacher feels most competent to handle. The television lesson on *Hamlet* is shown in October, but the classroom teacher does not receive the books and recordings from her department chairman until February.

When a television series is prepared for national distribution, it is unlikely that it will correspond exactly to locally conceived units of study, especially if the local curriculum is textbook centered. This criticism of television is at the same time one of its great strengths: the opportunity to broaden the scope of a subject far beyond that which any single school could provide.

Those who hesitate to use television lessons sometimes offer as an excuse the fear that there will be domination of their curriculum by outsiders, by those who would indoctrinate students on some nation-wide basis. Yet these same critics accept without question textbooks and films prepared by outsiders for national distribution.

Solution. Justifiable criticism of the content of television lessons can, for the most part, be overcome by having "grass roots" participation in lesson planning and by having an effective feedback system between the classroom and the producer of the television series. Effective productions are based on the needs and suggestions of the classroom teachers who will be receiving the lessons.

Such critical evaluation and assessment of needs can favorably alter the curriculum far beyond the areas directly affected by television. The Chicago junior college teachers who prepared the content outlines for the television series reported that they also reworked their regular class content to an even greater extent. Television may indeed make one of its greatest contributions by motivating a re-evaluation of the content of a high school course to eliminate deadwood and to revitalize that which is retained as essential.

Teacher Attitude

A significant problem affecting the acceptance of television on the secondary school level is the attitude of the classroom teacher. The high school teacher is a subject-matter specialist and is less likely to welcome assistance in his major field than the elementary school teacher who may be responsible for teaching three or four subject areas in addition to art, music, and physical education.

In spite of reassurances that his position is not in jeopardy because of the television teacher, the kingdom over which he has reigned supreme and unchallenged has been invaded by another authority, who may be better trained, with much more time to prepare lessons carefully, and with professional assistance to make the lessons dramatic and exciting. Since he has been trained without television, has little or no guidance as to the proper way to use the television lesson and little or no say as to what the television lesson will include, it is no wonder that the classroom teacher harbors fears that he will prove to be inadequate and incompetent in this new learning environment.

The conscientious, capable high school teacher feels the pressure of preparing his students to meet examination requirements and to make high scores on college entrance tests. He is aware that much—too much—of instructional television is passive in nature, requiring only that students sit quietly and attentively and absorb. He may be unsure of his own ability to stimulate, motivate, and challenge the teenager, but he is even more unsure of the efficacy of instructional television.

Solution. These doubts and concerns of the competent, dedicated secondary school teacher challenge the producer of instructional television series to improve the presentation from the standpoint of the learner. Harold Wigren, Educational TV Consultant for the National

Education Association, says that learning from instructional television is likely to be more effective when "the program promotes inquiry, stimulates children to think critically, raises questions rather than gives answers, poses problems, opens up a large range of alternatives or differing points of view or ways of dealing with a problem."[4]

Improvement of instructional television series is one of the aims of the National Instructional Television Center, located in Bloomington, Indiana. Subject matter, production, and teaching experts view existing courses to assess their instructional effectiveness, accuracy, and technical quality. Courses are screened for suitability for national distribution. Efforts of this sort are improving not only the quality of television series but also their availability.

Improving the quality of instructional television programs will tend to alter teacher attitude. Further improvement will be assured if teachers can learn effective utilization techniques. No television lesson can be good enough to overcome the handicap of poor classroom utilization. The teacher can make or break the television program by his attitude alone. The student has little motivation to concentrate on a lesson introduced by a listless announcement, "Put your books away now. We'll have to stop for that television lesson." If a creative television teacher has incited some curiosity by posing problems to be explored, the enthusiasm is certain to be dampened by the classroom teacher's sigh of relief as he impatiently concludes with, "Now, let's get back to work."

The importance of the classroom teacher's attitude has been recognized by the National Association of Educational Broadcasters. The NAEB has prepared a series of films available in "utilization kits," which include a 16 mm. film of specific examples of recommended utilization techniques, pamphlets, guides, and related materials. Film No. 6 presents "Examples from the Secondary School." Many teacher-training programs now include preparation for using instructional television as an accepted tool in the classroom.

Too much emphasis cannot be placed on the necessity of adapting the television lesson to the specific class receiving it. The dictionary is a valuable teaching aid when it is used for the purpose for which it is intended, but its value would be open to question if the teacher asked the class to open their dictionaries and read them for thirty minutes. In the same way the classroom teacher, and only the classroom teacher, knows the needs and characteristics of a specific class and how the television lesson should fit into the learning situation for those particular students. The introduction to *Hamlet* might very well serve as motivation for a class to embark on creative writing projects, to analyze the play scene by scene, to compare *Hamlet* with *Julius Caesar* by acting out comparable scenes, or for artistically inclined students to design appropriate settings and special effects.

A teacher's effective use of instructional television is based on his realization of the new role of the classroom teacher. There was a time when the high school science teacher was an authority, a dispenser of information, a supplier of ideas and techniques. Now, research uncovers new knowledge faster than even the most alert and studious teacher can assimilate. It is said that in biochemistry alone the published research reports for one year would fill an eleven foot bookshelf. The realistic science teacher accepts the fact that he cannot know his field in its entirety. He must depend upon the assistance of teaching aids, such as instructional television, to keep the base of information as broad and as current as possible. Instead of the dispenser of knowledge that is constantly changing as the result of research, he is now a teacher of techniques and methods, a director of learning activities. By sharing the content responsibility with the television teacher and the vast resources available to him, the classroom teacher can devote more attention to the learning problems of individual students.

Certainly the teacher of high school social studies defines his role more realistically if he accepts as his colleague in the educative process the television teacher and the camera which can bring the world into his classroom and make social studies dynamic and contemporary.

FALSE EXPECTATIONS

Although the attitude of the classroom teacher is the key to the success or failure of instructional television, the greatest disappointments in this area have been the result, not of teacher attitude, but of false expectations. Too many secondary school administrators feel that if they can put the old wine in new bottles, excellence will be achieved, but they are discovering that the new electronic bottles only accentuate a static curriculum and uninspired teaching.

Long before the days of the coaxial cable the Roman writer and philosopher Seneca offered this sage advice: "No wind is good if you do not know to what port you are sailing." Secondary schools have sailed off in a dozen different directions without knowing to which port their instructional television was really headed. To some this innovation is a way to save money by letting a television teacher handle more students than a regular classroom teacher. To others it is a way to teach large groups of students in an auditorium or cafeteria or to provide instruction in areas which classroom teachers are not qualified to teach. The collection of impressive, expensive hardware is good publicity and proof that the school is progressive. The application of the software to the needs of the high school is given minor consideration. Research reports of "no significant difference" between televised and traditional instruction give educators another reason for "using" television without a clearly defined purpose justified by the evidence.

Advantages

GOOD TEACHING FOR GREATER NUMBERS

There are significant advantages to be gained by the effective use of instructional television in the secondary school, not the least of which is the ability to make the best teachers we have available to larger numbers of students. There is a wide range of differences between the competencies of the best teacher and the least effective teacher. If equal opportunity is to be provided for all students, then the best teaching must be available to all and not limited, as it usually is, to the 150 students who are lucky enough to be assigned to the best teacher in the school system.

CONTENT AND PRESENTATION

The presentation of the television lesson has numerous advantages over the best that an individual classroom teacher can find time to prepare. The regular high school teacher with five classes meeting five days a week cannot be expected to prepare a lesson with the concentration and thoroughness which the television teacher can devote to his thirty-minute lesson.

Furthermore, the larger number of students viewing the television lesson makes it feasible to employ resources that would not be available to an individual teacher. The police judge who would be reluctant to give up time to speak to a high school American problems class of thirty, is more likely to tape an interview on "The Citizen's Responsibility for Law Enforcement" when he knows he will be speaking to thousands of teen-agers. The "Writers of Today" series extends to all high school students who view it the inspiration and knowledge otherwise limited to a group of New York City school children lucky enough to have Walter Kerr interview Archibald MacLeish, Arthur Miller, Langston Hughes, or Robert Penn Warren in a high school assembly—an unlikely treat without the aid of television.

INDIVIDUALIZING INSTRUCTION

When the responsibility for instruction is shared with the television teacher, the classroom teacher has more time and a better opportunity to work with individual students. While the television teacher is introducing the slide rule to a mathematics class, the classroom teacher is free to observe at what point difficulty occurs or attention wanders. The reaction of individual students is an effective indicator of trouble spots on which he may concentrate as he helps those having difficulty. Incidentally, the teacher may improve his own techniques by observing student response to the televised presentation.

IN-SERVICE AND PRE-SERVICE TRAINING

"A teacher cannot live on hoarded intellectual capital," said Melvin Barnes, Superintendent of Schools in Portland Oregon. "He must have the incentive to keep mentally in tune with that which is new and changing. As long as he teaches, he needs the stimulation of other scholars in his subject field."[5] The average high school schedule does not provide time for teachers to observe their colleagues except on an occasional visiting day when model lessons are presented under less than typical circumstances. But the high school teacher can observe good teaching techniques as they are demonstrated by the television teacher. No one need ever know how much he has learned by watching the lesson his students are viewing; he can "save face" while profiting by this observation of a scholar in his own field.

The camera can go where the classroom teacher cannot go and can provide observation of new teaching techniques. Thanks to television, groups of teachers can observe language classes using the oral-aural method or a team teaching situation. Portable closed-circuit television equipment is used in many teacher training institutions to permit discussion of high school teaching techniques while the professor and his students observe a laboratory high school class in action. Preservice training includes the video-taping of the practice teacher working with a class. Playback and analysis in a seminar provide practical evaluation.

LEARNING RESEARCH

The teaching-learning situation has been the subject for much research in instructional television. Increased knowledge about learning situations in general has resulted from the experiments conducted to put television instruction on a sound psychological basis. Good teachers will find much practical help from research projects such as the following:

1. Experiment in the adaptation of the audio-lingual system of language instruction in television
2. Attention fluctuation and the recall of television programs
3. Interest factors in instructional television
4. Use of remote unit in teacher supervision
5. A study of realistically vs. non-realistically portrayed examples and of literal vs. non-literal examples illustrating a principle
6. Evaluating the effectiveness of self-evaluation of basic Speech students in improving delivery
7. Perceptual recognition of pictorial signs[6]

STUDENT RESPONSIBILITY

Television has forced many teachers to re-assess their role in the teaching-learning process, and the student has found that he, too, has a different role to play. He may not be able to ask questions whenever he wishes; he may not be able to have a point repeated; he may receive quantities of information in a short presentation. In one high school it was discovered that the students in a television typing class were typing faster and more accurately than their equals in a regular class with the teacher present. When asked for a possible explanation of this difference, one student answered, "When the teacher is here, we rely on his smile or frown to tell us if we're working hard enough. When there's only the television set, we have to give everything we've got to be sure it's enough."

INDEPENDENT STUDY

Instructional television should lead to a continuing interest in self-improvement and independent learning throughout life. Learning which is entirely dependent on the presence of a teacher and which is directed only toward a problem assigned by a teacher is not likely to continue after dropout or graduation.

The Chicago junior college television experiment revealed the intense motivation of students who had been unable to continue their education in the traditional way and were now pursuing courses of study via television while earning their living or keeping a home. It should be part of the school's responsibility to motivate students to learn after "commencement" and to teach them how to learn on their own.

High school students are now, in some progressive areas, permitted to individualize their instruction by using video-taped television lessons in individual study carrels or viewing rooms. By dialing a number corresponding to the concept or program they wish, they may work at their own level and tempo; for example, a televised procedure for threading a machine can be repeated as many times as necessary to master the procedure.

STORAGE OF TAPED LESSONS

High school libraries have increasingly become instructional media centers and now include among their resources video-tape storage of lessons and series. Print-oriented teachers are realizing how many resources other than books are now an important part of the storehouse of knowledge.

School systems are exchanging and sharing these taped television series through national libraries, such as the National Instructional Television Center at Indiana University and the Great Plains National Instructional Television Library at the University of Nebraska.

Patterns of Utilization

It is not the extent to which a high school uses television but the way it adapts television to its needs that is the measure of success or failure.

According to the Educational Media Study Panel, "Experience indicates that the most effective uses of television have been in situations where it has been combined carefully with other activities in a total learning situation, and where students were strongly motivated to learn from it."[7]

MAJOR RESOURCE

The patterns of utilization are as varied, or at least should be as varied, as the schools receiving the television lessons. In some high schools instructional television is needed as a major resource. In subjects for which no qualified teacher is available, or which are elected by a mere handful of students the television course can provide all or a major part of the instruction.

Small high schools can, with the use of video-taped television lessons, provide as extensive a curriculum as schools with large enrollments. A senior boy need not be denied the chance to take a course in physics or electronics just because he attends a high school of only 100 students with no teacher qualified to teach these subjects. If laboratory facilities are inadequate, television may have to substitute for the major part of the course.

SUPPLEMENTARY AID

In other schools instructional television is merely a supplementary aid to enrich the regular school curriculum. For instance, a well-qualified teacher of English can use to advantage television lessons illustrating drama or poetry by interviews with poets and scenes presented by professional actors. The science class can visit by television a remote chemical plant or a mine in Montana or watch a designer draw with a light pen in "The Computer Sketchpad" from the *Science Reporter* series. The social studies class can visit by television a Congressional committee at work or an industrial area of the country quite different from its agricultural neighborhood or view the lesson from Dr. Max Lerner's *Seminar on American Civilization* as he and a panel of students discuss "Minorities and Segregation."

If a closed-circuit system is available within the school, television can be used as a visual aid in a biology class, magnifying the teacher demonstration of a frog dissection to fill the 21-inch screen, enabling all to see clearly even the most minute detail. The television camera can be used effectively to teach the correct use of the microscope. As the teacher shows bacteria on a slide, the student adjusts his microscope until he is able to see on the slide the picture which corresponds to the one on the television screen.

The use of television as a supplementary aid is possible even when the high school is not served by an educational station. The commercial television networks provide free of charge teaching aids and supplementary reading lists to accompany many of their "educational" programs. Science, social studies, and language arts teachers can find many programs worth assigning to their classes.

Non-Classroom Uses

Once television has been accepted into the family of teaching tools, the high school soon finds many practical uses that are only indirectly related to instruction in the classroom and yet are important factors in the educational environment.

COUNSELING

Most secondary schools have fewer professional counselors than they need to deal effectively with individual student problems. A specialist in a particular field by means of television, can be available to several students at once. In the area of selecting a college and applying for admission, a classroom teacher cannot keep up with the changes, the procedures, and the requirements, but a series of television programs by one trained college consultant can assist parents, students, and teachers in this important endeavor. Hagerstown, Maryland, televised an entire series of counseling programs to the schools of Washington County.

Help for broken homes, social patterns for teen-agers, what the school expects of parents, or how parents can best work with certain types of problem children can often be handled more directly through a community-wide telecast than through conferences with the individuals concerned, who may be reluctant to make a conspicuous visit to the school.

UNIFORMITY

Standardized tests are not so standard when we realize how varied are the environments in which they are administered. One principal is calm, reassuring, and explicit in giving directions. In another school the test may be administered in an atmosphere charged with anxiety, tension, and uncertainty. A trained person can administer the test on television to provide identical directions for all students. New York City resorted to this method of administering the qualifying test for principals, for only in this way could they be given identical classroom situations with which to cope.

Foreign language tests vary with pronunciation and delivery of the teacher dictating the tests. Some high schools televise the foreign language placement tests to the junior high schools to be sure the dictation is identical for all.

In a state-wide network, or even in a single-school district, there are occasions when some procedure, regulation, or policy needs to be explained in a uniform manner to all the schools involved. Here television can provide instantaneous, identical descriptive material to achieve the kind of uniformity needed.

FACULTY AND STAFF MEETINGS

In large school systems much time is wasted traveling between schools for administrative meetings with the various faculties. The district superintendents and principals can initiate procedure, explain policy, make reports, and introduce new staff members from the television studio early in the year, long before they could travel to each of the schools involved. Faculties assembled in their individual schools can "tune in" the county or area superintendent for his presentation and then proceed to their individual programs without traveling across the county or state.

PROGRAMS

No high school has all the talent in staff or student body. When these resources are shared by television, the resources are multiplied to an almost unlimited degree. One high school has a music teacher whose hobby is collecting musical instruments, another has a Latin teacher who specializes in presenting Greek dramas with a puppet theater, and still another has a social studies teacher who spent the summer behind the Iron Curtain. Television makes it possible for all schools in the district to receive the contributions of all three of these specialists without requiring them to lose class time in traveling from school to school.

The Future

In 1961 Wilbur Schramm stated in the foreword to *Educational Television: The Next Ten Years:* "For many reasons this has seemed a highly desirable time to take a hard look at educational television and at the problems and potentialities in its future."[7] As that decade has now ended with plans for a nonprofit system of satellite television to provide a firm financial basis for nation-wide educational television, it again seems desirable to take another look at educational needs and the role of instructional television.

The use of a satellite to beam television programs across the ocean became a reality in high school educational television on May 31, 1965, when a French class at West Bend High School in Madison, Wisconsin, talked for an hour with a class at the Lycée Henri IV of Paris, France, via the Early Bird Satellite. Lee Dreyfus and Gary Gumpert of the University of Wisconsin were responsible for the planning and production of this international incident between two secondary schools. The possibilities of such exchanges were noted by A. G. Weiner, Principal of West Bend High School: "Communication by satellite in the future opens vistas for education in understanding the problems, traditions, and customs of our neighbors. I can envision schools equipped with the technical equipment that will enable a given teacher, in a matter of minutes, to contact a counterpart in almost any area of the world. With this kind of communication, I am confident, we can make great strides toward solving the problems of human relations."[8]

Obviously, flexible schedules, flexible buildings, and flexible curricula will be necessary if television is to achieve its highest potential in the educational process. Teachers and teams of teachers will have new roles. Students will have more responsibility for their own learning.

Dr. Glenn Seaborg, chairman of the Atomic Energy Commission, has defined an educated man: "He is alert to his responsibilities to all segments of society, and he is active—never passive—in their performance. He is learned, but also conscious of the stream of life. He is a proud part of the mass of humanity, and yet aspires to understand it better and to leave it some legacy of material, mind, or spirit."[9] The secondary school with that kind of education as a goal for its students welcomes television as one way to open the windows to the world and involve its students in the "stream of life."

CHAPTER 4

The School Administrator's Role

by

GEORGE BIBICH

THE ROLE OF THE ADMINISTRATOR in educational television is much the same as his role in other areas, except that he often has little precedent to follow. Each decision is a new one and often conflicts with the accepted practices and theories expounded by professional educators. Many times he has to accept trial and error and be satisfied with the "best one can do at the present time" as the answer to his query. However, if he possesses deep faith in others and is willing to accept the responsibility for his blind decisions, the opportunity to participate in an exciting adventure is assured.

In the 1950's the St. John Township Schools in northwest Indiana's Lake County lacked direction; our students and faculty were unmotivated because our administrators were not responding to the challenges of mid-twentieth-century education. (The St. John Township Schools became the Lake Central School Corporation in 1967; at the same time, Dyer High School was renamed Lake Central High School. When St. John Township Schools are mentioned, the reference will be to events that took place before 1967.)

The administrator, as well as the classroom teacher in a small school system, can adopt one of two attitudes toward educational change: He may read about it and accept the fact that we are in a period of change, or he may sit back and let someone else attempt something different. While change was taking place in surrounding communities, our system was content to stay where it was, using the tried, proven, conventional methods that were rapidly becoming obsolete.

A new administration, hired in 1955, realized that change can have its advantages. The administrator can conduct research, discuss change with his staff and faculty, try to anticipate advantages and disadvantages, and then, realizing that he may make some mistakes, delve into the many, often foreign, facets of something new and unpredictable. From 1955 to 1959, many hours of hard work by administration, faculty, and parents were necessary in order to elevate the level of education to a competitive basis with other schools.

The personnel of the St. John Township Schools was still not satisfied. Plans were immediately initiated to raise our standards to those recommended by the North-Central Association of Secondary Schools and Colleges. After two more years of hard work and change, we were accepted as a fully accredited member. We were in the midst of change, we were excited by the things we were doing, and we welcomed ideas, suggestions, and new possibilities.

Decision To Use Closed-Circuit Television

My background included no experience or training in the field of television, nor was I a confirmed advocate of its use as an educational medium. However, I was blessed—or cursed—with a Latin teacher, Louis Iaconetti, who had a background of professional study in radio and television, and practical experience in the operation of the Armed Services Radio Network. Mr. Iaconetti was enrolled in the doctoral program in radio and television at the University of Michigan and was thoroughly convinced of the educational potential of television. He did everything that he possibly could to convince me of its value, although I was somewhat conservative about introducing another unknown. It helps to have a man on your staff who is interested in and qualified in television and who can take over the responsibility for planning and organization. It becomes part of his job to make surveys; do some basic research; and talk to members of the faculty, students, and parents to determine the needs of the school system; and then follow-up with the actual planning and production. Lacking such a person, you seek outside help, talk to your audiovisual staff who have probably had some training in television, and ask your teachers to assist you in planning the television program for your particular school system.

Mr. Iaconetti secured copies of programs from other schools and presented his views on televised instruction at a teachers' meeting. Other teachers were interested in the possible applications of television in our schools. They asked, "How will we use it?" "How much will it cost and how will we pay for it?" "Who else is using it, and what are their accomplishments and their problems?" Staff interest gained momentum; the teachers were sold on the idea that we could have television and make practical use of it. We talked to P.T.A.'s and any other groups or individuals who would listen to us. Continued discussions and presentations proved fruitful, but the real push forward came when our Trustee, the head of the township school system, entered the picture. Don Moriarity, the Trustee, believed that any tool or device which could provide a better opportunity for children to learn should be available for their use. I had no choice but to continue to investigate the possibilities.

Early in 1958, Mr. Iaconetti and I discussed the potential use of television instruction in our school system with various members of the State Department of Public Instruction. Their response was not overly enthusiastic but neither was it discouraging. They admitted that Indiana was far behind most states in this endeavor and that someone should undertake a study of its value. They indicated that they would be willing to evaluate a reasonable proposal and provide help if they could.

It took a committee headed by Mr. Iaconetti almost a year to read, evaluate, and draw conclusions concerning the value of this new teaching tool. Teachers, administrators, and members of the community conducted frequent meetings to exchange ideas and feelings about educational television. Before any steps could be taken toward planning a closed-circuit television program, all doubts had to be eliminated from the minds of the people involved. That in itself proved to be a long and painstaking project, but in the end only a very small percentage of the teachers still questioned the validity of the proposed idea.

While the committee was conducting the use study, Mr. Iaconetti and I were studying equipment and installation costs. Each company representative had his own idea as to what we needed and each had a different basic list of the equipment we should buy. We asked a consulting engineer to give us an objective appraisal and his suggestions for minimum standards in equipment turned out to be far different from those proposed by the representatives of various companies.

Now that we had an estimated cost, which we believed was within our range, and a decision by our Trustee to proceed with the project, we advertised for bids on equipment and installation. At this point we ran into our first major setback. The Township Advisory Board, which, under Indiana laws, must pass on each expenditure of $2,000 or more, refused to approve the outlay for television equipment. Our approach was to fall back on our holding company, the original builders of our school, which had some uncommitted equipment funds available. Once convinced that our staff, students, and community supported this proposal, the holding company agreed to provide the money. The addition of matching funds under Title III of the National Defense Education Act provided the necessary capital to buy and install the equipment.

The equipment purchased consisted of two viewfinder cameras and all the accessory equipment to complete the audio and video chains. We purchased and installed microphones, amplifiers, receivers, lighting, a master antenna system, a distribution system encompassing 74 rooms and offices within two buildings—Dyer Central High School and Kahler Elementary School, and a parallel sound system enabling students in any classroom to direct questions to the teacher in the studio during a lesson.

The system was designed with enough flexibility to allow the origination as well as the reception of a program in any of the 74 rooms and offices, an arrangement which proved valuable in the teaching of art and science. The master antenna system was designed to enable the two schools to receive programs from the Midwest Program on Airborne Television Instruction (MPATI), the local commercial channels, and educational station WTTW in Chicago.

The following list contains the costs of the basic equipment used by the two schools in their venture into closed-circuit television instruction:

CLOSED-CIRCUIT TELEVISION SYSTEM
COST BREAKDOWN, 1958

1	MLA Broadband Amplifier		$ 142.50
1	MLF Power Line Filter		20.25
2	MDC-4 Line Splitter	$ 28.00	56.00
74	1401 Jerrold Top Offs	7.50	545.00
2	101AF TV Cameras	1,595.00	3,190.00
2	A1734 ½ " Lens	129.00	258.00
2	A069-1 1" Lens	98.00	196.00
2	A1693-1 2" Lens	89.00	178.00
2	201A Audio Video Mixer	422.00	844.00
1	17" Portable TV (Monitor)		169.00
1	505A Switcher		80.00
1	Sampson Tripod & Dolly		158.00
1	Hercules Tripod & Dolly		258.00
1	CR 1774 bud 36" Rack		44.27
2	535 Shure Microphone	42.63	85.26
3500'	RG 59U Cable	56.80/M	198.80
3500'	8735 Cable	30.00/M	105.00
4	Inter-Coms (Common Talk)	40.00	160.00
1	Ampex Tape Recorder		589.95
1	Ampex Speaker Amplifier		189.95
1	R.C.A. 77XL Microphone		172.50
	Installation and labor		1,500.00
		Total	$9,140.48

Receivers have not been included in the above listing of equipment because any good standard receiver will serve the purpose. The receiver should have a 21-inch screen at least; the speakers should be mounted in the front of the set, or accessory speakers should be used. The number of receivers will depend on the particular needs and the funds available.

Each school system must decide for itself what kind of equipment to buy. You get only what you pay for and if you try to trim your television budget to the bone, you may find that you and your staff are soon disappointed with the performance of your equipment. There are ways, however, of cutting costs without cutting quality. While it is not possible to build your own cameras, microphones, and cable systems, it is possible to save money on certain aspects of your television installation if you have imagination, ingenuity, and a good shop department.

The stand for our "boom" microphone would have cost more than

$600, but we built it for $24 in our high school shop. A very common device in television installations is a multiplexer, which focuses films, slides, and pictorial materials for broadcast. We made one for $11; our version does the same job as equipment costing up to $1,200. Our shop also constructed a "pole cat," a box with four permanent sides. One side exhibits the school's test pattern; another a movable directory of events; the third, the United States flag; and a fourth side is available for other information. Acoustical treatment of the studio was accomplished with government surplus material obtained from Camp Atterbury, Indiana; a drapery concern had quoted the price at more than $600.

Our cameras and other production equipment are operated by a group of eighteen students who expressed an interest in learning something about television. After seven or eight hours of explanation, demonstration, and actual use under strict supervision, they took over the complete operation. Student cameramen have often suggested improvements that were practical and desirable, and several changes in our programs have been made on their recommendations. Knowing that their suggestions are welcomed, they keep alert for further improvements in the program. Students should be selected with great care; they must be mature and reliable to be entrusted with expensive equipment.

Programming

Planning and working out the program schedule was the next major step. The television committee had a basic proposed course outline in mind, but final decisions had to be made on such matters as which programs would be used, which subjects were best suited for television teaching, which grade level was most receptive to this new method of teaching, which teachers would teach, who would construct visuals, and how much time should be allotted each teacher for planning for each telecast. These questions and many more had to be answered before a successful learning atmosphere could be achieved.

Our criticism of many of the school programs we evaluated was that they did not make enough use of the media. This fact played a major role in our decision to start telecasting three freshman academic subjects and elementary art. All programs were live telecasts and originated in the classroom. Each was distributed to at least two other rooms.

The elementary art program was an absolute necessity because we were unable to hire a qualified elementary art teacher. The primary teachers and the high school art teacher planned each lesson cooperatively. Demonstration and lecture were the responsibility of the art teacher, and follow-up and evaluation the task of the regular classroom teachers. A detailed instruction sheet was prepared ahead of time and was in the hands of all teachers involved. Preliminary preparation material needed for that day's lesson was passed out by the classroom teacher prior to telecast. The art instructor then proceeded with her lesson and demonstration. If students did not complete their work by the end of her lesson, the classroom teacher followed it through. By means of this arrangement we were able to provide three times as much instructional time for art with no elementary art instructor on our staff as we had the previous year when we had one.

After our first telecast in elementary art, a first grade teacher who had had thirty years of teaching experience said, "I never knew that there were so many visual aids available to me in my home." If she could learn from watching others, we all could. From that point on television became a daily routine in our school system. We have used it for group instructional purposes in mathematics, English, and biology on the high school level; language arts on the junior high level; and art on the elementary level; and for group guidance on all levels. Homeroom programs have been very well received.

TV Team Teaching and the Core Curriculum

During the 1961–62 school year, a freshman group of about 90 students, of average and slightly below-average abilities, took mathematics, science, and English by way of television. The students were given a series of tests before starting the project. Throughout the year the TV teacher prepared one very thorough lesson every day. The lesson was televised to all 90 students at one time, in three different rooms, from a centrally located studio. The students, using an intercommunication system, were able to call on the TV teacher during a telecast, ask questions, or even participate in a class discussion. Each of the three block teachers taught in a similar manner. On several occasions students were brought into the studio to participate in special telecasts; they aroused and maintained the interest of the viewing students, often more so than the teacher.

At the end of the year, achievement tests were given to the group to determine the advantages or the disadvantages of TV teaching. The TV group was compared to a group receiving conventional classroom instruction in the same subjects. The findings seemed to indicate that:

1. The TV block students were better note-takers than non-TV students.

2. The better students seemed to gain more from TV teaching than non-TV teaching.

3. The average and slightly below-average learned more from TV than non-TV, yet they did not achieve the gains of the better students.

4. The below-average and poor students did essentially the same, with a few isolated cases achieving less from TV teaching than conventional methods.

5. All students seemed to be somewhat aware of the lack of teacher-student contact regardless of the intercommunication system.

The following year three classes consisting of ninety-seven freshmen of average to slightly below-average ability were taught freshman English, mathematics, and science in a new manner. The three teachers involved in the experiment decided on several projects ranging from simple to complex, chosen so that English, mathematics, and science were incorporated in each project to demonstrate the importance of being able to use each subject in solving problems in the other areas.

The teaching team broke the projects down into the essential material to be covered, and each teacher decided how his subject should be related to the core idea. All the resources, materials, audiovisual aids, and books concerning the project were centered in the individual classrooms of the team teachers and used by the core students after they were divided into their specific committees and given their research projects.

Library books on the subject of the project were put on a reserve shelf; they were taken out overnight or used in the library by the committees or individuals. The groups were given a reasonable length of time to plot graphs and charts, compile statistics, and compose grammatically their reports on the different phases of their individual work.

When each committee reached a certain level in its research work, it reported to the other members of the three classes over TV. Each committee chairman, selected in the initial stage of the project by the students themselves, introduced the members of his committee. The students presented their materials and showed their drawings, graphs, and any other visuals they might have had. Each member of the committee, in addition to his contribution to the total research, kept a notebook containing the report, an outline of the work covered, notes, and any drawings that were used in his presentation.

The teaching team launched this program by experimenting with a limited project at the start; larger and more complex projects followed. In this manner they were able to discover problems and limitations before they became too involved. The first core, "Flowering Plants," exposed the students to outlining, proper note-taking, paragraphing, library research procedures, poetry about fruits and plants, panel discussions, laboratory techniques, ratios, percentages, graphs, making charts, and making ecological maps.

Some of the findings, determined by tests and observations, of our teaching team are:

1. The students seem to prefer the course being taught by the discussion method. It enables each student to make his contribution.

2. All student achievement seems to be improved, with the better students of the groups showing a slight edge over the poorer students.

3. The students who normally do the least amount of work in the conventional class situation are pressured by members of their committees to work harder.

4. Most of the students are aware of their responsibility to the committee and try to improve their contribution to the group.

5. On days when students are to be in front of the camera, they present a neater personal appearance (hair in place, make-up applied with care) and a general attitude of personal pride.

6. Supervision is still a problem when one of the teachers is required to be out of the room for any length of time. It is less of a problem in classes with mental ability groupings that are above average.

7. The core curriculum plan requires better and much more detailed planning in order for it to be more successful than the conventional method.

8. More material, books, visual aids, and outside resources must be made available for this method of teaching to be successful. The

teachers, librarian, and students must be constantly on the lookout for these aids.

After two years of experimenting with groups of average or below-average ability, we decided to use television in teaching English, algebra, and biology to a group of above-average freshmen. The format of televised instruction and team teaching remained the same as it had been in the previous two years. The above-average pupils in biology, algebra, and English did not particularly care for television teaching; they resented the loss of personal contact with the teacher even though we had complete intercommunication. However, follow-up evaluation indicated that they learned more detailed information and retained it longer.

Television and the Homeroom Program

For some time our homeroom period had not been serving the purpose for which it had originally been designed. A survey was conducted by teachers and a committee of students to determine if closed-circuit television could improve it. Here is a sample of one month's homeroom TV programs:

Mon. Jan. 28	Art Appreciation	Mrs. Smith
Tues. Jan. 29	Social Pow Wow	Mr. Mygrants and Guests
Wed. Jan. 30	Talk of the Town	Mr. Jones
Thurs. Jan. 31	Counselor's Corner	Mrs. Wease
Fri. Feb. 1	Music Appreciation	Mr. Jordan
Mon. Feb. 4	What's New in Books	Arbuckle, Robertson
Tues. Feb. 5	Social Pow Wow	Mr. Yates and Guests
Wed. Feb. 6	Week's News in Review	News Staff
Thurs. Feb. 7	Counselor's Corner	Mr. Eberly
Fri. Feb. 8	An Overall View of Our Schools	Mr. Bibich
Mon. Feb. 11	An Overall View of Our Schools	Mr. Bibich
Tues. Feb. 12	Social Pow Wow	Mr. Tennant and Guests
Wed. Feb. 13	Talk of the Town	Mr. Jones
Thurs. Feb. 14	Counselor's Corner	Mrs. Wease
Fri. Feb. 15	Music Appreciation	Mr. Jordan
Mon. Feb. 18	A Look at the Sectional	Mr. Robertson
Tues. Feb. 19	Social Pow Wow	Mr. Mygrants and Guests
Wed. Feb. 20	Basketball Sectionals	
Thurs. Feb. 21	Counselor's Corner	Mr. Eberly
Fri. Feb. 22	Youth Looks at Communism	Mrs. Wease

A few of these program ideas may fit into the curriculum of other schools, but each administrator must determine his own particular needs. Once the needs are known, planning and producing can start, but it should be borne in mind that the informative and enrichment values of the program are of much greater importance than having a program that is a production masterpiece.

Social Pow Wow

"Social Pow Wow" is planned by our Social Studies Department. Each week one teacher from that department is responsible for the production and acts as chairman on the air. The students are polled to find out what questions or problems seem to be of primary importance at the time. There is much better response when two or three different students are included on the program every week. Often the panel consists of students, teachers, and the principal discussing a major problem, with each participant free to propose his own point of view. The panel serves to stimulate the students to discuss their problems constructively, and to create a rapport between students and faculty.

News in Review

"News in Review" is an all-student program with a complete news staff, news announcer, writer, director, and announcer for commercials. It consists of an analysis of the most important news events of the week, chosen and re-written by the students. They are urged to look for pictorial material to enhance the presentation of the news stories. A weather analysis and forecast is given at the conclusion of each program.

Talk of the Town

Dyer and the neighboring communities of St. John and Schererville were established between 1850 and 1860. Many people living in these cities are the children or grandchildren of the original settlers, and can produce old pictures and scrapbooks that have been kept in their families for years. As guests on "Talk of the Town," they show their materials, discuss the history of the community and relate interesting tales they heard from their parents or grandparents. In addition to

providing valuable source material for the study of local history, the program creates a lot of good will between the school and the community.

In general, we have been satisfied with television in our homeroom program, and we keep trying new things while refining and polishing some of the old. The student body prefers the TV homeroom to the conventional homeroom program conducted by the classroom teacher, or to the use of this time as a study period. Television enables us to reach the people we want, when we need to, eliminating repetition of the material to different classes at different times. The students enjoy programs supplemented by visual aids such as slides, charts, and film strips, and prefer watching in their own classrooms rather than in a crowded auditorium. A twenty-five minute segment for certain topics is, however, a limiting factor. We have become very selective in what we try to put across in one program, and if it seems necessary, we follow up with a second broadcast rather than trying to cram too much into one program.

COUNSELOR'S CORNER

For the most part, our television programs in guidance have centered around the needs of the students at a particular time. It has not been difficult to think of programs. Guest speakers have been very accommodating. The first program was a discussion of our testing program, test interpretation, and the terms used in this field of study. We had just finished administering a battery of tests and were preparing to interpret the results to individual students. Naturally the interest regarding this matter was high at the time, and subsequently many self-referrals were made. This response increased our enthusiasm and made us feel that TV could enrich the guidance program. Other guidance programs we have presented include:

1. Occupational information—How to use it and where to find it in our school. TV made it possible to acquaint the students with our career file and how it can be used. All students had a front row seat in seeing the usefulness of this guidance resource center.

2. Eighth grade orientation. Two forty-five minute telecasts designed to acquaint students in the elementary school with our high school program, classes, and extra-curricular activities were used as background for individual conferences with eighth grade students and their parents. High school registration was held a week later.

3. College outlook. Guest speakers, Professor Tackett and Dr. Trumpe of Purdue University, Calumet Campus, discussed college entrance requirements.

4. How the high school record applies to work and college applications. Actual applications were used as visual aids to make the program more meaningful. Using an actual permanent record card, we showed the students where and how information requested on the application blank is obtained.

5. A discussion with the principal and superintendent concerning student responsibilities and accomplishments. School spirit seemed to need a boost at the time.

6. Job opportunities in the 1960's. Mr. Montague of the Indiana Employment Security Division was our guest speaker. We were able to visit the homerooms receiving the telecast and make personal observations of student reaction to this program.

7. A follow-up of the above-mentioned program seemed necessary; by means of charts and graphs we discussed more specifically the outlook for certain occupations.

8. General Information program. Such topics as summer school and grades were discussed. A request was made for additional information from the students concerning awards received, offices held, and clubs that each had participated in during the year.

Preparation of a Typical Telecast of Counselor's Corner

The initial ideas for our programs are based on the recognized needs of our students as well as on referrals from teachers and students. With several possibilities in mind, the counselors carry on the discussion and make up tentative sketches of a program. After the initial plans are made, more specific details are worked up. The visual aids are probably the most important part of the program. While they need not be elaborate, these aids must be concise and must emphasize the major point. The lack of color adds to the necessity for careful planning. We sketch our ideas and students in the art department and mechanical drawing classes make the final copies.

The TV director is then sent a complete outline of the program for the week. A standard form for the television programs must be turned in to the TV room no later than 2:30 on the day before the telecast.

DYER CENTRAL HIGH SCHOOL
DEPARTMENT OF TELEVISION EDUCATION—PROGRAM WORKSHEET
D.C.H.S. T.V. SCHEDULE

Name of person or persons in charge of program ___Wease___
___Eberly___

Type of program ___Testing Program and Test Interpretation___
Title of program ___Counselor's Corner___

Equipment needed (*circle*): film strip projector, taperecorder, record player, (charts) (drawing space) picture holder ___easel___
Other

Number of persons that will be on mike ___2___

Names of persons needed in studio during program other than camera operators. ___None___

General outline of program (please list in order any pictures or charts that you want to use)

Introduction
Purpose of program (from desk)--Eberly
Description of program (from desk)--Wease
Testing program (display of test booklets,
    charts at easel)--Eberly
Explanation...using drawing at blackboard--Eberly
Briefing of test profile at blackboard using
    graph--Wease
Summary (from desk)--Eberly
Sign off....

About ten minutes before air time we go over the program for the last time. Total preparation time probably equals the time needed to prepare for a daily class assignment and is well worth it. Taping our programs has proved to be an effective means of evaluation.

Evaluation of Guidance Programs

From discussions of our guidance program with the faculty, with the guests who have appeared on the programs, and with the students; from questionnaires which have been sent to all members of the student body; from playbacks of our tape-recorded programs; and from personal observations, certain general assumptions can be made about television and guidance:

1. TV has offered us an opportunity to express publicly our role and our concern about each student. It is very gratifying to be approached

by a student saying, "Yesterday on TV you said. . . ." "I wonder if you have a minute to talk with me." TV has been a tremendous selling point for our guidance department.

2. We should utilize more students in our telecasts. To date, we have relied primarily on adults.

3. Students have requested more programs centered around one specific occupation. While a particular student may not be interested in today's program, eventually we will present the area in which he is most interested.

4. The faculty has been a great help not only in suggesting ideas for future programs, but also in reporting feedback from programs already presented.

An important asset of our guidance program has been provided in the form of closed-circuit television. At first the faculty had some doubt and apprehension about the effectiveness of this medium, but the faculty now believes that TV has great possibilities and that one of its strongest contributions can be in the field of guidance.

TV and Student Teaching

For several years we have been assigned at least three practice teachers per semester from Indiana State University or Valparaiso University. The future teacher meets frequently with his critic teacher to discuss subject matter, lesson planning, and teaching methods. He is expected to visit his critic teacher's classes, as well as classes of teachers in other departments. Eventually, he takes complete control of a class in his subject area. At this point, the critic teacher merely recommends, advises, or answers any questions the practice teacher might have.

Since we have started using television in our school, the practice teachers assigned to us not only follow the normal program, but they are also expected to participate in the television program. Whether they have the opportunity of teaching a class, or of participating in several special programs, all the beginners spend time in front of the TV cameras. Before they appear on television, they are given instructions about graphics, actions in front of the cameras, and studio cues; and a general idea about the function of the equipment. Naturally they approach the first telecast with some fear and apprehension, and invariably their preparation is not long enough to cover the allotted time. Fortunately, an intercommunication system from the receiving student to the teacher enables the teacher to initiate a question-and-answer session for the remaining time.

The practice teachers agree that after the initial concern about teaching in front of a camera is overcome, there are certain definite advantages to this experience:

1. The practice teacher must have a better and more thorough preparation when teaching on television.

2. He learns to anticipate questions or difficulties the student might have concerning a lesson and takes steps to eliminate them.

3. In our system, he is thrown in with other television teachers working perhaps as a team, or on a specific program. He is made more aware of the other teacher's problems.

4. He gains more self-confidence for entering a profession where television and other teaching tools and machines are available to the instructor.

Television experience is most valuable in the final preparation of the young teacher. Television is coming into greater use on the educational scene, and will some day be a part of the school day of every boy and girl in the United States.

From Closed-Circuit to Broadcast Television

When the New Lake Central High School was designed, studio facilities and a multi-channel microwave system were included in the plans, so that neighboring school corporations could receive our signal. Several superintendents expressed an interest in using our programs and sharing the costs. Dale Hartzler, the State Director of Television Instruction, suggested that we might look into the possibilities of matching funds for equipping an ETV Station, under the Educational Television Facilities Act of the Department of Health, Education, and Welfare. If H.E.W. matched the $108,000 already budgeted for an all-school microwave system, an open-circuit broadcast channel could be put into operation. The studios that were to be used for the microwave system could be easily converted for open-circuit broadcasting. With broadcast television all of Lake County, rather than just our school system could be served.

It took us eight or nine months to gather the information required by the Federal Communications Commission and the Department of Health, Education, and Welfare in order to apply for an educational television station. One must submit a thorough evaluation of need for educational television broadcast service in one's area; a detailed proposal for broadcast service, that is, short-range and long-range program plans; a list of the project apparatus necessary for the television station; and proof of legal and financial qualifications. (We had a problem with the legal qualifications section of the application, because we were a school township, and because we were building under Indiana holding Corporation laws. After much correspondence and much delay the Attorney General of Indiana rendered the opinion that "Indiana law authorizes a school corporation to own and operate an educational television transmitting station.) In preparing an application for an educational television station, you should get four people to help: a lawyer who specializes in broadcast matters, a good consulting engineer, someone who has already put his own ETV station on the air, and a Trustee like Louis Cinko, who is a champion of its cause. Several educational and civic organizations promised their support, and in April, 1966, the St. John School Township of Lake County, Indiana, (now the Lake Central School Corporation) was given permission by the Federal Communications Commission to activate ETV channel 50, under the call letters WCAE (Calumet Area Educational). At the same time a grant up to $109,000, on a matching basis, was approved by the Department of Health, Education, and Welfare for equipping the station.

Equipping WCAE–TV

Several factors had to be considered in purchasing equipment. First, it had to be compatible with standards established by the Federal Communications Commission. A second consideration was cost. Naturally, we would have preferred to have color equipment, but the price of two color cameras alone would have cost more than our budget of $218,000 for the entire station. Since our program director's experience was nontechnical, we asked Duane Weise (former Director of Maintenance and Operations for the Chicago Educational Television Association), our engineer consultant, to help us decide on the equipment that would serve us best. We reminded him that students would be using it. He recommended that first we hire the chief engineer who would put the station together and operate the equipment that students could not handle. Mr. Weise felt that the engineer's preferences should be a consideration in the final decisions on equipment, towers, tape recorders, cameras, and a transmitter.

Transmitters tuned to specific channels are not a stock item. At the time we were looking, a transmitter in excellent condition and of the power we desired became available. This transmitter was specified to all bidders on equipment. We located a professional type of video-tape recorder, and chose plumbicon cameras, a relatively new state of the art, as far as camera tubes were concerned. We accepted the Raytheon bid over other companies because the builder of Raytheon camera equipment was located within fifty miles of our station, the camera was in our price range, and the engineer we hired was familiar with this camera and had actually built a part of the central equipment for it. We located a used tower as well as a high gain antenna which was already tuned to our frequency.

When the bid was let in November, 1966, we expected to be on the air by March 1, 1967. Because of the Vietnam situation, however, electronic equipment and other materials, containing copper were becoming extremely scarce. One 325-foot continuous piece of 3½-inch copper feedline going from the transmitter to the antenna was lacking. Parts for rebuilding the transmitter were also slow in arriving. Personnel for installing the tower and antenna were rare, and once located, extremely independent. Finally on September 20, 1967, we received approval from the FCC. In the fall of 1967 test patterns were broadcast to show potential subscribers the quality of the reception they would be getting.

Looking Back

Television has given us a better understanding of the job that needs to be done, and its use has coordinated the effort. The staff is much closer together in its approach to helping boys and girls grow up. Each teacher's enthusiasm grows with the amount of involvement, and acceptance of closed-circuit television as a teaching tool has grown since its installation. Closed-circuit television has been a great time-saver, particularly in reaching large groups.

Television in the classroom has made the student a better-rounded, well-informed individual. He receives better planned and better organized lessons by instructors teaching over television; he is able to view telecasts of major importance or interest presented over local educational or commercial channels; and we are now able to have in our studio such guests as members of the community, personnel from colleges and universities in Indiana and surrounding states, representatives from industry, placement bureaus, and employment agencies, and professional athletes.

Television has given our student body a sense of responsibility and obligation. Through various weekly programs, students now have a voice in the school government. They appear on panels with teachers and discuss school regulations and general policy with the proper administrative personnel. The entire student body or just one class can watch the proceedings. Students having particular talents appear periodically on programs planned solely for entertainment. The whole school can enjoy the talents of the gifted and the performer gains confidence.

The fact that we are pioneers in television usage in Indiana has given our students and the community a feeling of pride in our schools. Our school system is recognized state-wide as one of the finest, and has been mentioned in national education bulletins and magazines. It has aroused the interest of fine young job-seeking teachers who have heard about our efforts in new areas and would like to be part of our system. We feel that our experiment with television has been successful and has brought about many changes in our school. Television will play an important role in future educational developments; its potential is limited only by the imagination of the user.

CHAPTER 5

The Television Teacher

by

BONNIE GILLIOM

A BOLD NEW VENTURE precisely describes the situation confronting a teacher when he first accepts the position of teaching on television. The purpose of this chapter is to suggest an itinerary for the adventurer into the world of instructional television. The itinerary consists of the qualifications he needs to bring with him from the classroom and from his own personality, the orientation he needs before he sets out, the roads he can take in becoming a professional telecaster as well as a professional educator, the steps he must take for evaluating himself and his series, and a few tips for getting along with the natives thrown in for good measure.

One of the more recent innovations in education is the television teacher. Notice the innovation is the teacher, not television, not even television-by-satellite. As far as education is concerned, television is just another powerful teaching tool, another McGuffey Reader or motion picture projector. Just as in the case of these earlier teaching aids, the ultimate success or failure of instructional television is largely controlled by two factors: the utilization of TV by the classroom teacher and his students, and the effectiveness of the TV teacher's presentation. Instructional television, having no magical educational qualities, is simply another medium of communication between intelligible transmission and intelligent reception. As a TV teacher steps before the cameras for the first time, he is accepting the responsibility for using a powerful tool of transmission through which his contribution to the learning processes of his students can be immense—or wastefully inconsequential. The end product is up to him just as it was in the classroom. The difference is quantitative rather than qualitative. In his new role as television teacher, the number of students he influences is greatly multiplied; hence, in the numerical sense, his responsibilities are greatly multiplied. Qualitatively, his responsibilities are unchanged; he will attempt to bring the best educational experiences possible to his students. In this effort, however, his day-to-day routine and duties as a TV teacher will differ vastly from his classroom teaching experience.

Characteristics of a Good TV Teacher

In answer to the prospective television teacher's question, "Will I be a good TV teacher?" I have a rather flip, thumbnail rejoinder. "Do you have a bit of gall, a thick skin, and an extra portion of poise? Pass these tests first; then, we will consider more serious qualifications."

THE FIRST TESTS

It takes gall to say to oneself, "I am a good enough teacher to teach thousands of students instead of the conventional thirty to a class. I am not afraid to open the doors of my classroom to face criticism of my scholarship and teaching skills from educators, students, parents, or the general public. I am confident that I can step before the cameras knowing that my first through my last TV presentations must be excellent."

In TV there is no opportunity to start slowly, or nervously, or by being an ogre with the idea of relaxing in a couple of weeks. While these mannerisms may work beautifully or at least do no harm in the classroom, they spell doom for the beginning TV teacher. Why is this true? Think for a minute of the classroom teacher's security; he has impunity because he has a captive audience. Not so the TV teacher. He knows classroom teachers are invited to watch his series once, and that they are never (or should never be) required to continue using it. Thus the newcomer is faced with the necessity of being a professional educator and a professional telecaster from his first telelesson to his last, with the constant threat of losing his audience if he should slip.

The thick skin is essential to anyone in the public eye—and TV is certainly public. I recall with some amusement the crank letters and anonymous phone calls dealing with such pertinent items as how I should wear my hair or how the telecast health-science lesson on human growth and reproduction (which incidentally had been previously cleared through religious councils, parent-teacher organizations, and medical associations) was "dirty, morally undermining the youth of today, and furthermore, communist-inspired." The TV teacher, while being sensitive to constructive suggestions, cannot afford the time, energy, or mental anguish of being thin-skinned to the lunatic-fringe communications, nor, for that matter, can he be egotistically fed by requests for autographs, sophomoric crush notes, and the like.

The extra portion of poise is just as essential as the thick skin— after all, every minute on camera is an emergency situation. What does one do if a camera goes out on the air and his beautiful visuals are lost to the audience, or if a guest does not show up at the last minute.

Having honestly passed these tests, the prospective television teacher might next consider the following qualifications.

SUCCESSFUL EXPERIENCE IN CLASSROOM TEACHING

A television teacher has to rely on a sense of timing, emphasizing, and sequencing that is learned from face-to-face communication with students; he must also be able to relate to classroom teachers not as an actor but as a colleague, a member of the total teaching team.

WILLINGNESS TO LEARN NEW SKILLS

Smooth, natural-looking telecasting operates within a framework of certain physical restrictions new to the teacher. He needs to learn technical restrictions and he needs to know why they are imposed. The teacher with a "forget the show biz, I'm a teacher" attitude is not the best candidate for TV teaching.

CREATIVITY, IMAGINATION, INVENTIVENESS

The ability to sense and to make use of the distinctive advantages of TV as a teaching medium is a real asset which may be developed.

It is, however, more likely to come already seeded in the teacher who has been frustrated in the classroom by lack of time, money, and facilities, but who has never given up trying new approaches to overcome these hazards. A continuous striving to attain the full potential value of instructional TV rules out simply giving a classroom presentation before the cameras or even "gimmicking-up" a previously successful lecture.

KNOWLEDGEABLE, CONTAGIOUS ENTHUSIASM ABOUT THE SUBJECT MATTER

Knowing the subject is not enough. The successful TV teacher must be able to arouse excitement in the minds of students—bother them, stimulate their curiosity, challenge them, give them a glimpse of deep love for a subject—and achieve this without the telling facial responses on which classroom teachers depend so heavily.

THE ABILITY TO WORK WITH OTHER PEOPLE

The beginning TV teacher finds himself involved in a multitude of new relationships with station personnel, administrators, consultants, classroom teachers, community leaders, guests, and the public in general. Of these, perhaps the one requiring the most new insight is the relationship with the professional telecasters. Station personnel respect the teacher as an educator and do everything they can to convey his teaching personality intact; in return, they expect him to become acquainted with and respectful of the television medium and the specific facilities and methods of the station. Although a casual air pervades most studios, the TV teacher must realize that maintaining this atmosphere is a duty of those working there, and that he must do his part in helping to reduce the tension that exists as long as programs are being taped or going on the air. He must also become oriented to having no one pay immediate and undivided attention to what he is saying or doing, or so it seems. The world of TV— exotic looking equipment, cameramen, floor managers, soundmen, artists, lighting directors, scenic designers, announcers, directors, engineers—is a bustling and, at first, a distracting one. The sooner the teacher can understand or at least appreciate the role each plays in the close cooperation necessary for producing one smooth telelesson, the better the whole series will be.

UNDERSTANDING THE TEAM TEACHING ROLE

The television teacher's relationship with receiving classroom teachers is a crucial one. The acceptance of television by classroom teachers in most cases has grown steadily and in proportion to their degree of involvement with it. In areas where in-school telecasts have been used for several years, the original fears of teachers' being replaced by the "machine" have faded away and the concept of team teaching—of the importance of both the classroom and the TV teachers' new roles—is evolving. By maintaining a humble attitude, the television teacher can help overcome another common fear of the classroom teacher—that of being in competition with a "master" teacher, an unfortunate yet common term for TV teacher. Although the goals of the classroom and TV teachers are identical, their functions are distinctly different and afford no basis for competition. The TV teacher's role is to explain, to demonstrate, and to provide motivational experiences. He is a master presenter—authoritative, efficient, effective. He may be in competition with a good text or shelf of resource books, but not with the classroom teacher. The most difficult tasks in teaching remain those of the classroom teacher—identifying individual differences, arranging learning experiences around them, leading face-to-face discussions, and guiding students to learn.

The impact of ITV on teaching roles and functions can be summed up in I. Keith Tyler's statement, in a paper presented at the International Seminar on Instructional Television at Purdue University, October 12, 1961, that the television teacher:

> . . . is not a "master teacher" but rather a specialist in television presentation. He is a team member with the classroom teacher, and together they provide the environment for learning. . . . The introduction of instructional television involves severe readjustments on the part of the classroom teacher. He is forced to surrender a measure of curriculum autonomy for the advantage of a better organized course and for the authoritativeness, currency, efficiency and effectiveness in presentation. He is likely to be hostile to television to the degree that he conceives his principal role as that of the purveying of subject matter. If, however, he can redefine his role in highly professional terms as a manager of learning situations and counselor of learners, he will find that the transfer of responsibility for presentation to the television teacher provides him more opportunity for handling group and individual

learning activities. In consequence, he will derive more personal satisfaction and fulfillment.

AN EXCELLENT COMMAND OF THE ENGLISH LANGUAGE AND AN INTEREST IN WRITING

The necessity for a nearly flawless oral command of the English language by the TV teacher is obvious; the necessity for the patience and enjoyment to write it—and write it—and write it—is often a surprise. In the eighth grade health-science series, which consisted of four twenty-five minute telelessons per week for one entire school year, the volume of writing (scripts, manuals, letters, art requests, evaluations) was estimated at just under 10,000 pages!

A GENERAL RESONANCE OF PERSONALITY

Under this catchall qualification comes the teacher whose outlook on life reflects general intelligence, a good physical and mental health, a sense of humor, and true dedication to teaching. A paragon, to be sure, but as Robert F. Fuzy, program manager of Chicago's WTTW has said, "We are no longer worried about whether students can learn from a teacher on TV; instead, we are worried about whether the TV teacher can teach the students."

Orientation to Teaching on Television

Even if an administrator is fortunate enough to find a teacher with most of these assets, he still faces the problem of orienting the teacher in a very short time to the new skills of teaching on television. Simply asking a teacher to do the same things on TV that he did in front of his class is one of the most serious errors that has been made in the evolution of ITV. Yet what can the school administrator do? Usually he is not qualified to provide necessary consultation and advice for he has never had the experience of teaching on TV or training in TV techniques. Courses and workshops for preparing television teachers, while growing in popularity are still few and far between.

One solution to this problem is to turn the training of a TV teacher over to the producer-director who has been assigned to work with the teacher. The director and teacher can then begin at the start to build a relationship, based on their mutual respect, which may in the long run determine the success or failure of the telecast series.

In thinking of the many duties of a TV teacher, I cannot recall a single one in which my director did not assist me. True, my basic responsibility was content and his basic responsibility was the sequence and quality of the picture and sound that went out over the air. But how much more mutually satisfying and beneficial it was to be able to infringe a bit on the other's duties, to script and visualize and reinforce and argue and learn and rehearse together—and to send out finally our best joint efforts into the schools. The teacher who misconceives his role as being the final authority on every question—content, pacing, visuals, performing skills, or any picayunish detail for that matter—is not likely ever to achieve that necessary goal of being on the same mental beam with his director. A director's similar misconception of his role is equally disastrous.

The orientation period is the time not only for the teacher and director to begin relating to each other, but also for the director to introduce the teacher to the telecaster's art. Techniques of naturalness, pacing, controlling the voice, moving, sitting down, standing up, holding and placing objects, using pointers, interviewing guests, using monitors, dressing and making up for TV and devising visuals for optimum clarity and interest are basic units in his curriculum. The outcome of a successful orientation period is a teacher-director team ready and eager to begin a series in which the teacher is a professional telecaster as well as a professional educator.

Duties of a Television Teacher

The birth of an entire new series can serve as an example of the major duties of a television teacher. The funds have been provided; the teacher and director have been hired; the subject and grade level have been selected. The television teacher, already oriented to television performance techniques, becomes involved in structuring the series with a steering committee, planning and executing each telelesson within the series, supplying information to classroom teachers, and evaluating every phase of the operation.

STRUCTURING THE SERIES WITH A STEERING COMMITTEE

The steering committee for a TV series is usually composed of at least one classroom teacher who will use the series, one curriculum specialist, the TV teacher, and, occasionally, the TV director and an

administrator in charge of instruction. This committee's first charge is
to decide how TV is to be used. Is it to be total teaching, a major resource, supplementary resource, or enrichment?

Total Teaching. In the case of total teaching, there is no classroom
teacher, nor, in fact, must there be a classroom at all. A classroom
teacher has not been replaced. Instead, successes in direct teaching
have stemmed from using it when there is no classroom teacher available. For example, very small schools which enroll very few college-
bound students may use instructional telecasts in chemistry or foreign
languages for those two or three who need these courses and for whom
no teacher is available. Another example of effective direct teaching
is "Operation Alphabet," a telecourse designed to teach adults how to
read and write in the privacy of their own homes.

Major Resource—a case study. This type of usage can be defined as
using TV as the guiding influence for an entire course. Anywhere from
one to five lessons are telecast per week, each building on the previous
lesson; teachers and classes watch together. The telecasts are usually
timed so they fall in the middle of a class period, thereby allowing the
classroom teacher time to introduce the day's lesson before the telecast and to follow up the telecast with discussion and class activities.

Television was used as a major resource in teaching elementary
school Physical Education over WOSU–TV. In Columbus, Ohio, as
in most other school systems, there are no physical education specialists in the elementary schools. Although most schools have very
adequate facilities for physical education, more times than not in the
past, they were used for everything except educating the physical
side of the children. The majority of elementary teachers frankly admitted knowing very little about physical education and welcomed
any help available. Here was an extremely fertile field in which to
work—the one question being "How in the world do you teach physical
education by television?"

Two major purposes for such a course were readily apparent—to
provide in-service training for the teachers and to demonstrate valuable motor activities in such a way that they would stimulate students
to experience them.

One fifteen-minute TV lesson per week became the source of the
activities for the week. The television teacher used as demonstrators
(actually as visuals) anywhere from two to thirty-five students with
whom she had previously held two practice sessions in their schools.
On the first and second grade level, five or six simple activities were

shown, centering around a theme such as "The Policeman." On the third and fourth grade level, most lessons consisted of two or three dances, skills, or games. On the fifth and sixth grade level, several weeks were spent on the progression involved in one team game or self-testing activity. Methods of teaching were demonstrated incidentally for the classroom teachers, though care was taken to insure that student viewers were not merely observing another class in the studio being taught. Instead, the TV teacher taught "to the lens" and, consequently, to the viewers in the classrooms. During the telecast, little participation by the viewers, other than mental, was possible since the boys and girls were frequently packed into a viewing room. They could, however, practice small skills, such as moving the feet in a box step or gripping an imaginary softball, and student response was almost completely without self-consciousness.

The real value in these lessons was obtained in the follow-up, and the boys and girls were usually most insistent on trying out what they had seen. The teachers, armed with a manual containing complete instructions for every activity demonstrated on TV and suggestions for organizing their few minutes in the gymnasium, were much more confident in this previously foreign field. From the volume of manuals requested, these physical education lessons have been viewed and, it is hoped, followed up by nearly three-quarters of a million students scattered over the United States, via tape libraries.

Art, music, and foreign languages at the elementary level are also frequently used in a major resource sense—with the television teacher suggesting the curriculum.

Supplementary Resource—a case study. In supplementary TV, the teaching roles are reversed. The classroom teacher is responsible for structuring the course and teaching it day by day; yet he does not give up the best aspects of television. Once or twice a week he tunes in TV for materials supplementing his course—perhaps the TV teacher is taking students on a field trip or performing experiments for which the schools are not equipped. In a supplementary series, while teachers usually will want their students to view every telecast, they may miss an occasional TV lesson and still not lose course continuity.

The evolution of a series from major to supplementary resource may be seen in the story of eighth grade health-science in Columbus. A study group worked diligently on preparing a new two-semester required course for eighth graders to replace the unsatisfactory one semester of health and one semester of science previously required.

The resulting course guide, thick as a city telephone directory, seemed a masterpiece of curriculum engineering. No adequate textbook could be found, but the guide was so full of excellent resources that it was agreed a text was not needed. The only major setback occurred when it was discovered that very few teachers were qualified to teach the new course, which ranged from the study of optics through emotional disturbances, from sewage and water treatment through dating. Hence, the idea emerged that one teacher, freed from all other responsibilities, could develop a twenty-five-minute daily television series (major resource) as a step in implementing the new course. This teacher would provide the most vivid and accurate descriptions possible about health concepts in order to inspire the students to learn something about them.

The first year health-science was on the air, it began as a one-man operation. The TV teacher, using the guide extensively, established objectives, selected units, prepared the teacher's manuals, did research on each lesson, wrote scripts, and did his best to utilize the benefits of TV by devising good visuals and interviewing outstanding guests. He soon discovered two things—that he was working anywhere from sixteen to twenty hours daily and that many of the receiving teachers were not satisfied with the televised lessons. TV was new to them, no attempt had been made to define their responsibilities, and they felt little, if any, involvement in the televised course.

This reaction precipitated two important changes during the first two years of telecasting health-science. One was to lighten the TV teacher's load by bringing in a second teacher. The other was to hold several meetings a year with receiving teachers for purposes of evaluating past lessons, planning future lessons, and building the feeling that only through a carefully planned team approach could television and classroom portions of a lesson be unified into a meaningful whole.

By the end of the second year, reactions of the receiving teachers indicated that one purpose of the TV series had been fulfilled—the course was no longer new, and they were ready to take over the responsibilities of teaching it day by day. Yet they were hesitant to give up the best aspects of the series—the impact of Woody Hayes telling students to appraise their health, the excellent films available at the right times, the trips through the city's health and safety facilities, the microscopic slides all could see simultaneously, and the experiments for which their schools were not equipped. The conclusion was to switch from using TV as a major resource to using it as a supplementary series. This change meant decreasing the lessons from five to two per week and limiting these lessons to educational experiences usually beyond the potential of conventional means of instruction. I do not mean to imply that what was done on these supplementary television lessons could not possibly have been done in the classroom. Under the most ideal circumstances, perhaps one class could experience all these activities firsthand, and certainly the students in that one class would reap even greater benefits. Yet the limitations of time and budget alone in the conventional school would make this possibility extremely remote in the one class and impossible for all the classes in range of the signal.

Health-science as a twice-a-week supplementary TV course was used for two years and by the end of the second year, the series was outdated in several respects. References to the preceding year's exciting new discoveries in health and in science were, in fact, old hat in many instances. Current statistics quoted were no longer accurate. Even some first aid techniques demonstrated had been revised.

In remaking the supplementary series, another new approach was tried, based on student and teacher reactions. In an attempt to establish better rapport, one TV teacher rather than two now appears on camera. To determine more realistic needs, a classroom teacher who had used the series for three years, was assigned to work full time with the TV teacher for one semester in an attempt to redefine the objectives of the series, select units and topics to be taught, further clarify roles of TV and classroom teachers, prepare the calendars and manuals, and do research on each lesson.

At least three conclusions were reached during the development of health-science by TV: Most teachers adapt readily to the use of television if they become really involved with it and if it is adapted to fit their changing needs; effective use of instructional television results in a modification of the traditional role of the classroom teacher; and the greatest strength of this educational tool seems to lie in its ability to communicate vivid, accurate, and exciting materials to many individual students.

Enrichment. The fourth catchall classification of TV usage is enrichment. Just having TV sets in the classroom and turning them on during any of the Apollo moon shots enriched the lives of millions of students, and they did not have to play hooky for the experience. Under enrichment we could include also the in-service training programs designed for teachers to watch at school or at home. An example of this may be found in KQED's "Espanol Para Maestros." Over two thousand elementary teachers in the San Francisco Bay Area, armed with manuals and records, prepared to teach Spanish at the elementary level by watching this series.

After deciding on type of usage, the committee's second charge is to select the objectives of the series. If the sponsoring body has already developed and adopted a sound syllabus or curriculum manual for the course, the objectives can be taken directly from it with one addition. The series must provide valuable experiences for students that would be difficult for classroom teachers to arrange.

The third charge is the most difficult: selecting the scope and sequence of curricular units and determining the number of telelessons to be devoted to each unit. Here is the rub—and where the charges of lockstep curriculum and "teacher loss of autonomy" are fired. And here is where painstaking care must be taken to involve as many classroom teachers using the series as possible, to promote a better understanding of the changing roles of classroom teachers, and to assure classroom teachers that if the series does not fit the receiving class, the TV set can always be turned off.

The committee's last responsibility is establishing objectives for each lesson, set at teaching only one or two major concepts, but teaching them thoroughly and visually. They should be written out and everything in the lesson should relate to them.

PLANNING AND EXECUTING EACH LESSON

With the committee's suggestions in mind, the objectives established, and his enthusiasm sharpened, the TV teacher is ready to begin formulating a telelesson. How thoroughly he prepares each lesson in advance will partially determine the effectiveness of it. The teacher starts with an idea, the source of which has been the interaction of the committee. He begins building a mental picture of the entire lesson—concentrating not only on what will be heard but also on what will be seen by student viewers. He makes use of the extra time assigned television teachers for research, and digs into libraries, newspapers, magazines, historical societies, museums, art galleries, public relations departments in industry, and any other place that may be a potential source of information, material, or visuals. He finds, often to his surprise, that community resources are vast and merely waiting to be tapped, that the general public is anxious to help him find exciting materials, and that busy people are delighted to take time out to help him prepare a telecast.

Formulating a Verbal-Visual Outline. When he is satisfied that he has combined all sources, the TV teacher divides his lesson idea into its important steps to develop an outline. This outline includes both the verbal and visual elements of the lesson. Indeed, the seasoned TV teacher tends to think in two columns—one audio, one video.

SAMPLE WORKING OUTLINE

Series Title: *Health Science, 8th Grade*   Taping Date:
Program No. and Title: #6, "Defects of the Eye"   Air Date:
Television Teacher: Mrs. Bonnie Gilliom   Guests: None

Video	Time	Audio
Get an apple, a model jet plane, and a kitten. Devise a way to show a shaft of light shining on an object seen by my eyes.	3:00	1. Motivation (book opening) Have students form a mental picture of an apple, a jet plane, and a kitten. Compare their mental image with realia. Why so close? Mind is a storehouse of things seen in the past. What is necessary for seeing? 1. Light. 2. Object to be seen. 3. Eyes.
	1:00	2. Outline of lesson (aid note taking) Put an outline of the lesson on magnet board. Review structure of eyes; explain causes and corrections of two major defects—nearsightedness, farsightedness.
Get an orange and an eye model. Find & clear that good film clip comparing an eye & an orange (write narration).	2:00	3. Review structure of the eye. Compare eye and an orange.
Have camera on long shot go out of focus. Get a nickel (to read fine print). Devise a chart showing normal, nearsighted, farsighted eyes. Make rays of light of	4:00	4. Explore nearsightedness. How does a nearsighted person see? Distance fuzzy. Close things plain. What causes nearsightedness? Defect in shape of eyeball; compare to normal eye. How can nearsightedness be corrected? Double concave lenses; show

Video	Time	Audio
elastic cord so they can be manipulated. Get a large double concave lens. Manipulate chart to show correction.		realia. Put cardboard lens on chart, move focal point to retina.
Have camera with close up shot of nickel out of focus. Use chart again, get a newspaper. Get a large double concave lens. Manipulate chart to show correction.	4:00	5. Explore farsightedness. How does a farsighted person see? Distance plain. Close things fuzzy. What causes farsightedness? 1. Defect in shape; compare to normal eye and to nearsighted eye. 2. Age—demo moving newspaper back to read it. How can nearsightedness be corrected? Double convex lenses; show realia. Put cardboard lens on chart, move focal point to retina.
Wink.		6. Closing. Importance of eye examinations. Look into other defects and diseases. Be good to your eyes. They're important.

Since television is a visual medium, the television teacher cannot utilize it to the maximum unless in his original planning of an individual lesson he thinks in terms of strong visual elements. Visuals are not gimmicks or gadgets to be dreamed up after a script is written and learned. Instead, they must be natural and an integral part of the lesson. Unless they strengthen the point being made or motivate further interest, they are meaningless.

Among the many visuals a TV teacher may locate or devise, some of the most valuable are films and filmstrips, slides, printed materials mounted on flip cards, boards, superimpositions, crawls, lighting effects, and guests. While the obtaining of exciting visuals is one of the joys of TV teaching, it is also very time-consuming and frequently becomes tied up in red tape.

1. Films and filmstrips. Standard 16-mm. films or filmstrips may be used effectively within a lesson to illustrate a point, tell a story, or lend authenticity. To make use of films or filmstrips the teacher must

go through the following steps: determine what films or filmstrips are available, preview the best of these; select the most pertinent one, book it; get copyright clearance on it; edit the desired sequences (using a complete film or filmstrips is often a waste of valuable television time); time the sequences to the second and determine a precise cue line; and determine whether to use sound-on-film or voice-over to best integrate the clip into the lesson.

If no pertinent film is available or if a timely local event is to be covered, an original film can be made. A local field trip with the teacher involved as a guide is an excellent use of original film. The steps in this process are very time-consuming and the teacher must plan thoroughly in advance to get permission to make the film from the owner or manager of the site, develop shot sequences on paper, travel with the photographer to the site, have several takes of each sequence photographed, allow time for developing, edit and time the sequences, and study the film carefully so coordinated narration may be given.

2. Slides. Two-dimensional visual material may be presented on 2 x 2-inch transparencies or slides. It is essential that the slides are in a horizontal rather than a vertical format because a portion of the picture content of the latter is lost if it is to fill the entire screen. Any photograph or anything which can be photographed can be prepared as a slide.

3. Flip cards. Pictures, clippings, diagrams, cartoons, graphs, and other illustrative materials may be mounted, printed, painted, or drawn on cards, preferably eleven by fourteen inches. The power of a picture story on flip cards should never be underestimated. With proper timing, narration, and, perhaps, background music, a picture story can be one of the most powerful devices available on television. On the other hand, a television teacher who relies primarily on an occasional picture on a remote flip card to "spice-up" his lesson is not beginning to achieve the potential benefits of television.

4. Boards. Magnet boards are the most popular type of board used on television today for manipulative purposes. These are porcelain-surfaced green chalkboards on which chalk may be used. Their extra value lies in the steel base to which magnets will adhere. Papers, cutouts, words, and pictures with magnets taped on the reverse side may be displayed and easily rearranged on the board surface without tacking, taping, or in any way marking or defacing them. Flannel boards

and spaghetti boards (such as are often used in cafeterias to display menus) are also useful for displaying and manipulating visuals.

5. Superimpositions. Visual information from two or more sources can be superimposed. This technique corresponds to what photographers call a double exposure. In television, it is accomplished easily and inexpensively by having two or more cameras on the air at the same time, producing one image superimposed upon another. Superimpositions are widely used in news programs and interviews. A person's name, in white letters, is "superimposed" on the TV screen.

6. Crawls. A crawl is a device commonly used in commercial television to superimpose titles and casts of characters in a smooth flow from the bottom of the screen to the top. Printing or any other two-dimensional visual material can be attached to a long roll of paper which will be revealed, then disappear in sequence before the camera's lens.

7. Lighting. Various dramatic effects can be achieved through lighting. Exaggerated contrast and lowered intensity may be used to make highlights stand out and dark objects disappear. A projection microscope image thrown on the wall of the set can be picked up by the camera when studio lights are turned out. A light box with two 60-watt bulbs behind a translucent glass plate can be used as a background for silhouettes or acetate overlays. An overhead transparency projector can be very valuable in a television lesson if the studio lighting is dimmed.

8. Guests. While it may seem strange, guests, too, may be considered as visuals, and the use of guests—real authorities who are too busy to visit individual classrooms—is one of the foremost advantages of instructional television. In many cases the guest is more expert than the teacher in a particular field and will add to the information presented to students. Guests can also add importance to information. The teacher could read John Ciardi's poems on television, but were the poet to read them himself, the chances are the attitudes, understandings, or values of listeners would change considerably more.

When the decision has been made to use a guest, the very best person available should be asked. Almost without exception, the busiest and most authoritative people will be glad to share their knowledge and experience with students via the camera.

Writing a Script. Every television lesson requires a written script or "run-down" indicating both the visuals to be used and the sequence of ideas to be expressed. Usually scripts or run-downs are due a week in advance of airtime so the director and other crew members can have ample time to prepare to follow the presentation. The type of scripting may vary from an outline to a fully written, exactly worded manuscript depending on the method that best enables the television teacher and his director to think alike.

Not only is scripting essential for content, smooth presentation, and clarity of thought, but also for instructions regarding demonstrations, use of visuals, planned movements, and all important cue lines. The script is the final form of the lesson—and the best form of communication between the director and the teacher when on the air. It is essential that the television teacher stay with the script, even if a point he had forgotten to include in the script happens to occur to him during the TV lesson.

The opening should be friendly and eye-catching. A "hook" open (an interest catcher) is very effective if it pertains to the lesson, strengthens it, and is not overdone. A picture story, a riddle, an interest-catching visual, or any good motivation that might be used in the classroom could be an effective opening.

Within the lesson, the teacher should break his remarks into short units. The viewing eye finds it very difficult to hold a static object for long—and interest will wane. The teacher must keep the viewers in mind as he prepares his script to keep it on their level of understanding and keyed to their interests.

In closing there is one basic rule to follow—leave the lesson open-ended. A pat summary of all that has been said can leave the student with several wrong impressions such as "Class is over, now I can sleep" or "That is all there is to know about the atom." Summarizing by taking a new view of material plus questioning or challenging the students makes the transition from the television to the classroom portion of the lesson more natural and places responsibility for further investigation on the viewer.

The most common television script form is divided into two columns. The left third of the page is the video column, the right two-thirds of the page is the audio column. Although the video column is used by the director for marking camera shots, the teacher is responsible for indicating in this column such information as desired framing—CU APPLE (close-up of an apple), LS MARY AND LARGE

CHART (long-shot including Mary and all of the chart), FILM (3:00), FLIP CARD, and other visual materials. These instructions are typed in capital letters across from the corresponding spoken segment. In the audio column, word-for-word spoken dialogue is typed in lower case letters. If only headings are used, they are typed in capital letters. Instructions for music or sound effects, also typed in capital letters, are included in the audio column.

SAMPLE SCRIPT

Series Title: *Health Science, 8th Grade*   Taping Date:
Program No. and Title: #6, "Defects of the Eye"   Air Date:
Television Teacher: Mrs. Bonnie Gilliom   Guests: None

Video	Time	Audio
		(All spoken lines in lower case; all actions, descriptions in upper case)
CU MODEL OF EYE	OPEN-ING :30	MUSIC UP AND UNDER
SUPSLIDE (Health Science) SUPSLIDE (Mrs. Gilliom)		
DIZ TO TALENT (chest shot)		MUSIC OUT
	1:30	Good morning. Today's lesson will be devoted to a study of the human eye, but before we begin, let's try a little experiment. I'm going to mention three different objects, and as I name them, I'd like to have you form a mental picture of each. So—ready . . . here they are. An apple . . . a jet plane . . . and a kitten. Now let's compare.
CU APPLE ON COUNTER		Did your *apple* look at all like this one? It probably did—big, round, red . . .
PAN RIGHT TO CU PLANE ON COUNTER		And how about your *plane* . . . was it a sleek, silver beauty like this, perhaps streaking through the sky?
PAN RIGHT TO CU KITTEN ON COUNTER		And surely the kitten you pictured was nearly identical to this one. (Ad lib)

Video	Time	Audio
MS TALENT AND COUNTER		Now how could this be? How could these words call up such accurate images for you? Isn't it because you have seen apples, planes, and kittens many times . . . and that your mind has stored away these mental pictures?
		But what if you had never seen an apple, a jet, or a kitten? What if you had been blind since birth? How then would your mind picture them? With sight, your mind is filled with pictures of every kind . . .
LIGHTS OUT (OR TAKE BLACK)		without sight your brain would be imprisoned in/ total darkness.
CU SPECIAL DEVICE		Actually, there are only three ingredients necessary for sight:/
BEAM OF LIGHT	1:00	1. *Light* is the source of all seeing. Without light, you'd see no more than a blind person does.
TILT DOWN TO VASE OF FLOWERS		2. An *object* to be seen is essential. Light, then, hits the object and is reflected from it to the . . .
DOLLY BACK TO INCLUDE EYES OF TALENT MS TALENT		3. *Eyes*, which are body organs that transform light into nerve impulses./
		These then are the ingredients for sight. Today's discussion will concern just one of these—the eyes. In our next lesson, we'll talk about light rays. To aid you in taking notes, I'll put an outline on the board. Please leave space for your notes./
CU MAGNET WORDS		

	:30	I. Structure of the eye
		II. Defects of the eye
		   A. Nearsightedness
		     (Myopia)
		   B. Farsightedness
		     (Hyperopia)

When the script is constructed from the outline, transitions should be worked over until they are right. Thinking in terms of how students will react makes subordinate items fall into place. Notations should be made between the audio and video columns as to how long each segment will take. Timing the parts keeps the whole lesson more easily in proportion and finished on time.

The television teacher must have complete control of the last thirty seconds of his lesson. He must know in advance what he will say when he sees the thirty-second signal. It is wise for him to prepare a pad and a cut in case of emergency—once again, so he and his director are thinking alike.

Off-Camera Rehearsing. The process of lifting a script off the paper and coordinating it with action is a difficult task. By having the script and visual emphasis organized in a logical pattern, the teacher does not need to memorize every line of a script. His responsibility is to know the sequence of units and cover each within set limits of time. To check himself, the teacher needs at least two run-throughs by himself (or preferably with the director) prior to the day of the telecast to work out any problems that may arise.

Although some teachers have found that audio-tape recording a rehearsal is a valuable check of voice and content clarity, others believe this method has a stilted carry-over effect when the teacher goes on the air. Some teachers find that giving the lesson before a live class prior to giving it on television helps greatly in pacing. Others find rehearsing before a mirror adds to confidence. But whether off-camera rehearsing is done at home, in an office, in a classroom, or in the studio without cameras, it is the teacher's last chance to evaluate his planning and make necessary changes.

On-Camera Rehearsing. Once the cameras are turned on, the rehearsal is no longer for the benefit of the teacher. Instead, it is strictly for the benefit of station personnel. Here the director, floor manager, cameramen, and audio and video operators are checking out every shot and every movement. The teacher may be asked to start and stop many times, skip units and return to them. A complete uninterrupted run-through is seldom accomplished. The teacher must understand that this is a process to acquaint a large crew with exactly what will be going over the air—not to iron out his problems and especially not to make last-minute changes.

SAMPLE RUN-DOWN SHEET

Series Title: *Health Science, 8th Grade*   Taping Date:
Program No. and Title: #6, "Defects of the Eye"   Air Date:
Television Teacher: Mrs. Bonnie Gilliom   Guests: None

Video	Time	Audio
		(All spoken lines in lower case; all actions, descriptions in upper case)
CU MODEL OF EYE SUPSLIDE (Health Science) SUPSLIDE (Mrs. Gilliom) DIZ TO TALENT (Chest Shot)	OPEN-ING :30	MUSIC UP AND UNDER MUSIC OUT
CU APPLE ON COUNTER PAN RIGHT TO PLANE PAN RIGHT TO KITTEN	1:30	Good Morning . . . apple . . . jet . . . kitten . . . Now let's compare. SHOW APPLE SHOW PLANE SHOW KITTEN
MS TALENT AND COUNTER LIGHTS OUT (OR TAKE BLACK)		How could this be? . . . without sight your mind would be imprisoned in/ total darkness.
BEAM OF LIGHT TILT DOWN TO FLOWERS DOLLY BACK TO INCLUDE TALENT MS TALENT	1:00	1. Light 2. Object 3. Eyes . . . WALK TO MAGNET BOARD
CU MAGNET WORDS	1:00	ingredients for sight . . . outline on the board . . . Leave space for notes./
MS TALENT		I. Structure of eye (review) II. Defects of eye—nearsightedness, farsightedness/
CU EYE MODEL AND ORANGE FILM #1—VOICE OVER		WALK TO COUNTER Famous doctor story . . . definition of verb to review . . . new view of structure of the eye by comparing/ an eye and an orange./

Video	Time	Audio
	2:00	An orange is very much like an eye . . . Here then is the complete seeing mechanism of the eye; the cornea, the iris, the pupil, the lens, the retina, and the optic nerve./
CU EYE AND ORANGE ON COUNTER		
MS TALENT		The next time . . . recall how it resembles an eye./
	:30	The first defect . . . myopia . . . to a nearsighted person, TV often looks
ON AIR CAMERA—OUT OF FOCUS		like this/—all blurred and fuzzy . . ./
ON AIR CAMERA—BACK IN FOCUS		Interesting fact . . . read fine writ-
EXTREME CU NICKEL ON COUNTER		ing inscribed on this nickel/
MS TALENT		AD LIB/
	1:00	What causes myopia? TALENT WALKS TO LARGE CHART Normal eye
CU CHART—TOP ⅓		is nicely rounded/ Compare this to
PAN DOWN—MIDDLE ⅓ OF CHART		the nearsighted eye/. . . The cibary muscle can't accomodate the lens to throw the focus point back to the retina where it must be for clear
MS TALENT		vision./
	:30	A defect in shape of eyeball . . . not cured . . . corrected TALENT WALKS BACK TO COUNTER Corrected by
CU LENS ON COUNTER		double concave lenses./
MS TALENT		DEMO LENS ON COUNTER/
		Let's put a double concave lens in front of the nearsighted eye TALENT
CU MIDDLE ⅓ OF CHART		WALKS TO LARGE CHART/

1. Using memory aids. To guarantee that the teacher and the director are thinking alike and that they move unerringly from one point of emphasis to another in the proper sequence, it is usually necessary for the teacher to use a prompting aid of some kind. These aids range from a word-for-word typewritten text that unrolls through a lighted viewing box near the lens, to one small note card with four or five key words on it. In using the former, the teacher must be certain that he does not appear to be reading. In using notes, he may organize the material on 3 x 5-inch index cards which can be handled easily,

quietly, and often off camera by framing the teacher just above the notes. Cheat sheets, too, may be helpful, and are simple for the teacher to prepare. These are large cards on which key phrases are hand written in oversized letters; they may be held next to the camera or taped on it. If both cameras are to be used as cover cameras, then duplicate cheat sheets should be made to tape on each camera.

2. Understanding cues. During a telecast there is no verbal communication with the teacher, yet he must receive and react to necessary signals and cues pertaining to timing and action from the floor manager. It is not necessary to acknowledge cues; indeed, the viewing audience should never be aware that signals have been given. The teacher is responsible for prompt reaction to them even though he may not be able to see why he must make a certain move or fill an extra minute.

Time signals are usually given by holding up cards on which large numbers indicating remaining number of minutes are printed. The floor manager communicates other information to the teacher by using standard hand signals for "stand by," "you're on," "look at the other camera," "the close-up is on," "speed up," "slow down," and "move closer together." Often the floor manager will have to improvise cues such as "move back so I can remove this rug," or "rearrange the articles on the desk," or "your guest has finally arrived and will be in in two minutes." The teacher's peripheral vision in receiving these cues is his safeguard to a smoother performance.

Performance Techniques. Nearly every performer on television experiences a case of program jitters and often this is a wonderful aid. The extra adrenalin pumped into the body serves to sharpen the mental process. Even so, errors are bound to occur, and by correcting them in a natural or humorous way without calling undue attention to them, the teacher becomes more human and likable. By being well prepared, the good television teacher can be more relaxed, natural, convincing, enthusiastic—a professional doing justice to both education and television standards. I recall many lessons or performance techniques that I learned from trial and error and from my first television directors; I shall list those which were most valuable to me in acquiring some insight into the telecaster's art.

1. Naturalness. Perhaps the most helpful single suggestion is that the teacher should remain perfectly natural. Not everyone knows how to play this role. Often it is the untrained person doing the work to

which he is accustomed who achieves the highest level of performance. The worst pitfall for a novice teacher is the tendency to imitate
an admired radio or television personality. When this does not work,
in an effort to be himself, he then tries to "sell himself" as a package
of carefully rehearsed charm and wit to the exclusion of the subject
matter. As every teacher should know, students are as astute in de-
tecting insincerity as they are in responding to genuine enthusiasm.
One advantage in communicating real sincerity on TV is the ability
of the TV teacher to look directly into the eyes of every student watching. His attention is no longer divided among his thirty or forty classroom students. He can talk easily and directly to each viewer by looking into the on-the-air lens of the camera. To lessen the chance of a
cold delivery to a cold piece of equipment, some teachers think of one
particular student whom they are trying to reach; others visualize two
or three students as if in a post-class discussion with them; still others
teach to the cameraman behind the on-the-air lens. I personally found
myself drawn to the lens as if it were an open hole into the mind of a
receptive being, quite possibly my own mind. Whatever the method
used, real intimacy can be achieved by teaching to the lens as if to a
friend—never staring it down, yet never forgetting it.

2. Pacing. A sensitive classroom teacher seldom has difficulty presenting his subject matter at a pace proportionate to his students'
understanding, since he can read their expressions and answer their
questions as he goes. The television teacher does not have this opportunity, just the memory of it. In addition, he has the problem of the
static image. Eyes within the classroom are fixed on a small non-
moving area—the TV receiver.

A general rule for TV unit length is between three and five minutes;
at the end of each unit, some change in physical setting or mental
processes should be introduced to keep the viewer's attention. TV
can manipulate viewer attention, eliminating the extraneous and distracting elements found in the classroom and focusing on the "meat"
of each unit. The problem of pacing then becomes one of holding
each visual experience long enough to be comprehended, anticipating
difficult and complex points, remembering previous student questions
and responding to them, and pausing verbally to allow for appropriate
student responses, both mental and physical. Silence is not deadly on
television and is often very effective.

3. Voice. A normal conversational speaking voice is adequately
powerful for audio pickup, since an engineer controls the volume

which goes out over the air. He cannot, however, control the pitch of the voice, and many novices as well as seasoned television teachers will find that the slight nervous tension during a telecast will raise the pitch of the voice considerably. Women, especially, need to listen to their own voices and force them into a lower range if the pitch becomes unpleasant. Breathiness, another sign of nervousness, can be alleviated by breathing deeply and swallowing several times before going on the air.

One cautious note should be remembered—there is always a chance that a studio microphone may be turned on, either on the air or into another part of the station. Care should always be taken to avoid extraneous or perhaps embarrassing conversation within the range of a microphone.

4. Moving. All movements of on-camera people can be natural, but they must be deliberate. Extremely fast movement should be avoided or the person will find himself off camera. The director must be aware of the move about to be made and where it ends so he can forewarn the cameramen, and moves should be indicated both on the script and by the teacher's verbal or visual cue.

In walking to a chart, chalkboard, rearscreen, or other object which is to be seen in a close-up, the teacher should stand as close to it as possible without having a nose or shoulder in the close-up shot. Care should be taken not to step in front of the close-up in moving to another spot before the cover shot is again taken.

Although natural gestures help to give life to a presentation, they should be used sparingly when a chest shot of the teacher is being taken. Arm waving, head bobbing, seat shifting, and foot swaying are mannerisms that may drive cameramen to distraction and show only portions of the teacher.

5. Holding objects. Another of TV's foremost advantages is the ability to magnify, to fill the screen with an extreme close-up of material which could not be seen more than a few feet away in the classroom. The picture and printing on a postage stamp, for example, can fill the screen and be seen by all in the classroom at the same time. A very small object can be hand held by the teacher and should be whenever possible to identify the object with the teacher. Then students and teacher take a close look at it together. It is essential that such an object be held as still as possible by steadying it on a prearranged spot since the slightest movement will be greatly magnified on the screen.

6. Using pointers. Using a pointer scaled to the size of the visual is preferable to using the hand in a close-up for practical as well as esthetic reasons. It avoids the possibility of blocking out the visual, guarantees clarity in a detailed chart or piece of equipment, and gives a degree of motion to a static image.

7. Placing people. When two people are in one shot, they should stand only a few inches apart. Awkward as this may seem at first, it makes a better picture composition on the screen with less wide open space between faces. If a teacher and his guest are seated, a good arrangement is putting the chairs at an angle so over-the-shoulder shots may be taken.

8. Using the monitors. Studio monitors are placed within viewing range of the TV teacher expressly for the purpose of enabling him to check whether viewers can see what he wants them to see in a close-up. Only after the tally lights on the cover camera go out should he check the close-up on the monitor. All too frequently, the teacher is guilty of monitor watching—of making quick side glances in the direction of the monitor throughout the entire lesson. When carried to extremes, the teacher ends up teaching to the monitor, thus losing the valuable assets of eye contact and intimacy with the students.

Supplying Information to Classroom Teachers

A major responsibility of the TV teacher is to supply information to each receiving classroom teacher. An introductory letter should include the days, time, and length of telecasts; for whom they are designed; the purposes of the series; how the series is designed to be used; an invitation to watch the series regularly; and a request for criticism of the series from the classroom teacher.

A year's calendar of the series giving the title and a brief description of each program should be in the classroom teacher's hands in the spring prior to the start of the series. This timing enables him to make plans, order films, schedule field trips, and make other arrangements during the summer "vacation"—all of which will further meaningful utilization of the telecasts.

Finally, and most important, the classroom teacher needs a detailed manual at least one month in advance of the telecasts described within. Preferably, he should receive a complete manual for the year just prior to the start of the school year. The minimum information contained in a manual should include objectives for and a thorough outline of each lesson. To insure better utilization of the lessons, the manual may contain suggested activities for use before, during, and after each telelesson; a list of resource materials that will assist the teacher in using the lesson; and concepts the television teacher assumes the class already has mastered. The format of the manual for the major resource elementary physical education series for example, included the following for each lesson:

I. Objectives for the week.

II. Suggestions for pre-telecast activities.

III. Outline of the telecast.

IV. Instructions for activities demonstrated on the telecast.

V. Suggestions for post-telecast activities in the classroom immediately following lesson.

VI. Suggestions for post-telecast activities in the gymnasium or on the playground.

VII. Tips for teachers.

The effectiveness of television lessons depends ultimately on how well they are used in the classroom. The time-tested educational principle, "learning is doing," need not be violated through passive listening and watching of a television lesson. In the first place, a student giving careful attention to a telelesson is involved in covert participation and may be furiously arguing, thinking, and evaluating during the lesson, and, in the second place, he may become overtly active if the TV teacher and classroom teacher together use one of the following participation techniques during telecasts:

1. Give the class an oral or written quiz.

2. Ask for a show of hands and a tabulation of them.

3. Have the class repeat words, phrases, or definitions.

4. Have one or all of the class sing, speak, dance, or play a game along with the teacher.

5. Have the class handle materials, such as paints, clay, rulers, or worksheets which have been prearranged on their desks.

6. Have the class outline or take notes of the telecast.

7. Have the students refer to their books or to a map or to common objects in classrooms.

8. Have a class begin a project to be completed after the telecast.

9. Call on (TV teacher) and evaluate the answer (classroom teacher) of a specific person, i.e., the girl closest to the front and the windows.

10. Ask the classroom teacher to call on one or more students to answer a question, demonstrate an exercise, point out selected items on the screen, or summarize the lesson.

Several avenues of communication between the classroom teacher and the television teacher should be kept open; among these are telephone calls, postcards, monthly or yearly group meetings, workshops, and visits by the television teacher to the classrooms. In communicating with classroom teachers, the television teacher must maintain the highest professional standards in accepting criticism gladly even if it is not of value. The television teacher visits classrooms to see what happens to the students, what contributes to the learning process, and what hinders it via television; to discuss with the classroom teacher ways in which to improve the course; to give assistance to the classroom teacher whenever possible; and to become a "real" person to the students.

EVALUATING THE SERIES

If both television and classroom teachers are to continue to use television, constant evaluation must be carried on. To be valid, the evaluation must be based on the established objectives; anything that measures their achievement becomes an instrument for evaluation. Situations can be created so that students can demonstrate the effectiveness of the television-classroom lessons. After they have had the opportunity to demonstrate behavior changes, an interpretation of the responses in light of the objectives must be made and a report of the evaluation given to students and teachers. By using this framework of evaluation, meaningful changes can be made either in the teaching approach or in the evaluation procedures.

Specifically, the television teacher or a television coordinator may elicit evaluation of telecasts through a feedback card or an interview situation regarding the clarity of objectives; interest, involvement, and comprehension of students; organization of lessons; satisfactory sound and picture; and overall impressions of the lessons.

Why Teach on Television?

Some of the television teacher's duties have been outlined in the preceding section. Never are they in such an orderly sequence—nor as cold and impersonal as they may sound. A typical day (taken right from my calendar) might run more like this:

7:15 A.M. Pick up porcupine at zoo

7:45 Pick up kitten at veterinarian's

8:00 Camera rehearsal, Science #82, "Structure and Function of Hair"

8:30 Tape Science #82

9:00 Evaluate tape with director and curriculum specialist

9:20 Visit Everest High School, watch Science #76 in classroom

10:00 Visit Come Elementary School, hold rehearsal #1 for Physical Education for 5th and 6th series, "Basketball" lesson

11:00 Return animals, make next four school appointments, and call Civil Defense director

12:00 Lunch meeting with director, discuss remote basketball lesson

1:15 P.M. Visit Sheldon Elementary School, hold rehearsal #2 for Physical Education series for 1st and 2nd, "The Farm" lesson

3:00 Finish writing Science #90, "The Nervous System"

4:15 Turn in art request on Science #88, "Respiration," see carpenter about building model

4:30 Mail February manuals, write thank you notes to teachers

In my opinion, it is a wacky kind of life! Why be a TV teacher? Extra money? No! Extra time? Yes! Time to plan, to dream, to do new things, to do research never before possible, to meet experts and authorities in their fields, to do the best job possible! The optimum formula is one hour of preparation for each one minute on TV. Miss the students? Yes! But how many more students can be reached.

I recommend TV teaching as one of the most stimulating and exciting positions in the world. And one of the most pleasantly exhausting!

CHAPTER 6

The Television Administrator

by

E. DANA COX

THE TELEVISION ADMINISTRATOR is concerned with program selection, course development, financial matters, scheduling, personnel policies, coordination with school administrators and teachers—in other words, handling the thousands of details which occur in any kind of educational administration. He must be able to anticipate, provoke, and communicate ideas; to work under pressure without showing signs of pressure; and to create an atmosphere of mutual understanding and respect. The administrator is truly a coordinator of time, sight, and sound.

In a large educational television station there may be a staff of fifty or sixty people, including a general manager, a program supervisor, a director of promotion and publicity, a director of in-school services, a chief engineer and his staff, writers, producers, directors, secretaries, bookkeepers, and various part-time helpers. But in the small closed-circuit television system one man may serve as general manager, program supervisor, writer, producer, and director. If he is lucky, he will have an engineer to supervise technical operations, but the rest of the technical and production staff will probably have to be recruited on a part-time basis.

The role of the administrator in television production and programming obviously varies from station to station and from school to school. Rather than deal in generalities, it would probably be more helpful to talk about specific practices and policies. Throughout this chapter references will be made to some of the operations at Station WBRA-TV and the Blue Ridge ETV Association, Inc., in Roanoke, Virginia.

Responsibility to the Community

The administrator of an educational television station must make every effort to be an active member of his community. Through first-hand involvement in civic improvement, the social and cultural life, and long-range community planning, he becomes sensitive to the needs and problems of the community. His programming should reflect the needs and interests of all the people within range of the broadcast signal. His knowledge and concern, however, must transcend the borders of the station's signal area. He must be aware of national and international problems and issues. These questions can and should be expressed on a local level, and can be made relevant to the lives of persons in the broadcast community.

Keeping a pulse on the community—its strengths and weaknesses—can offer rich rewards for the TV administrator. Many times problems can be aired and brought to the attention of the community long before the problems become issues. The administrator who has a firm knowledge of the community is constantly on the alert for such program potentialities.

Responsibility to the Schools

One of the important functions performed in any station is that of in-school services. Approximately thirty percent of the total operational revenue of an educational television station is derived from them. Although most stations employ the services of an in-school coordinator to act as a liaison between schools and station, the administrator has the responsibility of establishing policy which directly affects school services.

The TV administrator should be familiar with basic learning theory, he should realize the broad problems of education, and he should be aware of the needs of the school systems within the primary coverage area of his station. For example: Is the teaching staff strong in the social sciences and humanities, but weak in science and mathematics? How many teachers of art, music, and physical education are in the system? Would in-service programs for teachers be helpful, and if so, who should be contacted for further exploration and discussion? Are the schools well equipped with audio-visual aids, including television receivers? Are teachers, curriculum consultants, supervisors, and parents well informed about what services could be rendered by television?

I want to emphasize the word "service" here, because that is how we view our relationship with the schools. We try to understand the aims and objectives of the schools, and we try to develop in-school programs which will be meaningful, interesting, and rewarding for both teacher and student.

Course development varies from station to station, but at some point, curriculum committees usually come into play and have a great bearing on course development. Within the Blue Ridge ETV Association, Inc., an association comprised of nineteen school divisions, each division supplies one curriculum specialist in each area of course involvement. For instance, each division designates a teacher to serve on science curriculum committee. The obligation of this committee is to establish broad outlines which reflect the needs of the individual school systems involved. There is thus a composite reaction to nineteen specific needs existing in the broadcast coverage area.

These needs are translated into course content on a unit-by-unit plan. The exact content is not described in detail, however. Separate units are devised by the curriculum committee and are used in previewing existing prerecorded video-tape lessons. If existing materials fill the needs as reflected by the curriculum committee in this given area of science, then prerecorded materials are used. If no adequate material exists, the broad outline established by the curriculum committee is used to derive basic guidelines for studio teachers.

Auditions are then held at WBRA-TV, the Blue Ridge ETV Association, Inc., station, to find a studio teacher competent in the subject area to develop course content and curriculum materials following the instructions of the curriculum committee. The selection is a very important decision, and the TV administrator must be well acquainted with the art of communications. He judges prospective TV teachers on their communication abilities and on how well they will meet the receiving students' needs. The temperament, disposition, capabilities, and limitations of each teacher must be evaluated and considered before the administrator can assign a producer-director to work with the television teacher. To choose a producer-director who would not be compatible or complement the teacher would not be in the best interests of the instructional aspects of the station. Strong directors with leadership capability held build confidence, poise, and a strong sense of purpose in the TV teacher, and thus strengthen the televised lesson. Although the TV administrator is not present when a given lesson is transmitted from the studios to the classroom, his effectiveness in choosing personnel is measured as a positive or negative reaction in the eyes of the receiving classroom teacher and student.

Developing a TV Lesson

Before the TV teacher–TV producer team even thinks about a television studio, they should spend many hours talking about course objectives, course content, teaching methods, and methods of evaluation. Only when both have the objectives of the course clearly in mind, should they begin to think about the medium of television. Many questions have to be considered: How can certain concepts and ideas be visualized? Are there any ideas or concepts which simply cannot be visualized? How can you maintain personal contact with students when there are no students in a TV studio? The TV teacher and the TV producer must approach these questions and problems as a team—one is a content expert, the other, an expert in communications.

Using his knowledge of script, teacher, student, and cameras, the producer-director must design the lesson to eliminate meaningless movement. Each movement of the teacher must serve a purpose to accomplish a fluidity of the learning situation. Mannerisms which call attention to themselves and movements which are not motivated must be eliminated by the producer-director before presentation. When the teacher moves from one part of the set to another, the reason should be obvious or should be revealed soon after the movement. For example, the teacher stands in one portion of the set and poses a question. He pauses, giving the students a moment to react, says "Let's see," and moves to another part of the set to guide the students to a conclusion through the use of visuals. Movement should not break concentration but should enhance or serve to keep concentration at a high level. Movement should never be distracting but should be strong and made with conviction. Just as stage movement is made with and for a purpose, movement on the television set should be staged and well planned.

In the theater the viewer's eyes can roam about the stage to concentrate on the significant or be drawn to a distracting influence. Through camera selection—shot sequences—the producer-director is essentially the eyes of the student, for he selects what the student will see. His decisions must take into consideration the progress of the learning situation, the lesson content, and the logical sequence of meaningful images to be projected. The producer-director of a lesson must look at the control-room monitors with an eye toward the esthetic, but he must also imagine himself as the student in the very last row of the receiving classroom.

The producer-director, studio teacher, and artist have many conferences to determine the background or setting which will be utilized for the series. Before a final decision is made, the man in charge of set construction and the engineer in charge of lighting are brought to the conference to determine the overall feasibility of the design. The producer-director periodically checks the progress of the construction of the set and special materials to be used in the lessons.

The TV administrator works very closely with the studio teacher, the producer-director, and the curriculum specialist in planning a series of lessons. Film, if not available in existing footage, can be shot and inserted into lessons. Time-lapse photography, slow motion, or stop-frame projection are but a few of the techniques which the administrator and producer can suggest to enhance subject matter. Visualization of subject matter, whether in the form of 16-mm. film, still photographs, artists' drawings, or live cameras must complement the instruction being transmitted to strengthen the concept that the television lesson is providing instruction that is otherwise not available. The material received must offer a service that the classroom teachers cannot provide for themselves.

The creativity and imagination of the producer-director can contribute greatly to the final script that is prepared for the televised lesson. Although it is usually conceded that the curriculum specialist and the television teacher have autonomy in regard to lesson content and presentation, the guidance and leadership provided by the television professionals—the administrator and the producer-director—in the areas of visualization, lighting, sets, background, and movement are integral parts of the effectiveness of the televised lesson.

Utilization

The development of the subject area and assignment of the studio teacher and producer-director does not necessarily guarantee the success of the instructional lesson. Allan Stephenson, In-School Coordinator, WVIZ, the educational television station in Cleveland, Ohio, once told the following story to a group of classroom teachers to emphasize their position in the instructional lesson: A wise old man, widely known for his correct response to questions, had irritated a young man by his consistent wisdom. The young man, holding a live bird behind his back, approached the wise old man and said, "Wise old man—knower of all—I have a bird in my hand. Tell me if it is alive or dead." The young man had gathered a crowd for the event to prove the wise man wrong. If the wise man responded, "The bird is dead," a live bird would be produced. If he replied, "The bird is alive," the young man would crush it and produce a dead bird. The wise man thought for a moment, looked the young man in the eye, and replied, "Young man, the answer is in your hands."

No matter how well the instructional lesson is planned, the material prepared, and the teacher rehearsed, and no matter how well the producer-director has blocked, staged, or coordinated all aspects of the lesson, the overall results and effectiveness of the instructional lesson are "in the hands" of the classroom teacher. Utilization of the televised lesson is a very important facet of the total learning situation. The classroom teacher decides if the lesson will be viewed or discarded, and through his attitude student attitudes will be formed. Lessons can be viewed with no classroom follow-up and be ineffective, or the classroom teacher can reinforce the televised materials on the level of the individual student's need.

Utilization personnel and procedures vary from station to station. Educational television stations which contract for in-school services often have no personnel assigned, thereby leaving utilization to the school systems. Some stations have one person who meets with curriculum committees. From a position behind a desk high with papers, he receives calls of praise or complaints from classroom teachers but has little direct contact with them.

The most extensive utilization known to this author is that followed by the State of Georgia and designed by Lee Franks, former Executive Director of the Georgia ETV Commission. An entire department was established by Mr. Franks for utilization; it is supplemented by a mobile television unit that travels from school to school throughout the state. The mobile unit is connected to the distribution system of a school, and classroom teachers are involved with the actual creative process of the televised lesson. Studio teachers are available to assist and answer questions for the classroom teachers and to view the instructional lesson with students.

Utilization activities follow no established pattern and are shaped by the educational philosophy and the autonomy of the educational television station. The main purpose of utilization is to offer assistance to the classroom teacher and to provide an evaluation process for the effectiveness of the televised lessons.

Within the Blue Ridge ETV Association, Inc., the administrator joins the studio teacher and the in-school coordinator as a part of the utilization team. The in-school coordinator's visits to each school serve as a pulse for the station, so that frictions or problems can be made known to the station before they become issues. If problems arise with individual teachers, the coordinator can schedule a visit by the studio teacher. If there are problems or questions among many of the classroom teachers, area utilization meetings will be held involving all the school divisions within the locality. These meetings involve the studio teachers, the TV administrator, and the in-school coordinator.

The studio teacher also visits the classrooms throughout the broadcast area in an attempt to upgrade his lessons by viewing his instructional material. While viewing his lessons in the classroom, the studio teacher can better evaluate his effectiveness and obtain response from both students and classroom teachers. If the classroom teacher needs special instruction, the studio teacher is available.

The TV administrator or producer-director also visits the classroom to view lessons, and although he is also interested in lesson content, he is more interested in the production aspects of the lesson. His purpose is to evaluate the blocking, effectiveness of his camera placement, and the motivational aspects that are evident or lacking in the direction. Often in viewing lessons with students, the concepts and motivation which were planned in the studio do not evoke the planned response. Just as often a motivational or involvement factor is found that was not planned, and this concept can be used in succeeding lessons. In the area utilization meetings the TV administrator answers questions of scheduling, timing, and visualization, and makes mental notes for future production techniques. A report on these impressions is then given to additional staff members, and from this staff meeting the TV administrator determines whether the station's production facilities should be used for in-service utilization on the air. If the station is to be used for a series of programs on utilization information, the TV administrator handles the internal coordination in a manner similar to the instructional lesson.

Scheduling

As much flexibility as possible should be incorporated in the scheduling. The in-school lessons and evening programs should be considered as separate and distinct. Obviously, the educational television station, like the commercial station, is concerned with reaching the greatest audience possible with any given program.

The television administrator should have at his disposal the schedule of each school to determine how many students can be reached with a given lesson at a given time. Secondary school lessons should be offered at alternate times for flexibility of scheduling. The educational television station must offer as much versatility as possible, but individual secondary schools must also be willing to re-schedule and depart from tradition in order to obtain maximum benefit from available educational opportunities.

Each lesson offered at the elementary school level should be repeated at least once during the week at an alternate time period. Lessons for a given grade level should not follow each other immediately in the program schedule and thereby reduce the opportunities available to the schools. Thought should be given to the particular time of day so that the subject matter is received at a time when maximum effectiveness can be achieved. These considerations are based on information coming from the schools, the administrator's knowledge of the school situation, and his knowledge of the learning process.

The lunch period, which is difficult to program for elementary and secondary schools, is an ideal time to offer instructional television for the institutions of higher education. Since these institutions do not usually depend solely on assigned classroom time to view lessons, course offerings can be programmed during this portion of the broadcast day. The optimum time to repeat these telecasts is after secondary and elementary school hours and prior to evening community programming.

Financial Aspects

Most educational television stations are actively involved in soliciting funds for the year-to-year operation of the station. Some stations, and this is no accident, are quite successful in annual fund-raising endeavors. The most successful stations, and certainly those with the largest budgets, have involved local industry, civic groups, school systems—public, private, and higher educational institutions—in their financial structure.

Most educational television stations derive a portion of their annual operating funds from school systems on a cost-per-child basis. That is, a school, through some formula (membership on a given date, enrollment, or average daily attendance), is assessed a given sum per child, and in return, a systematic series of lessons is aired through the station's facilities for classroom instructional purposes. This contracted service usually includes the cost of manuals or curriculum guides for the classroom teachers.

Additional operating costs are derived from program underwriting. A good example is "The French Chef," featuring the culinary art of Julia Child, produced by WGBH, Boston. The series, which is distributed nationally, had a portion of its production costs defrayed by a large eastern chain of supermarkets. The TV administrator should recognize the possibilities of tying a program which is based on a definite audience need to a possible source of production or operational money; this combination of program need and financial procurement fosters and promotes an involvement which has great rewards for the educational television station.

Direct solicitation from the general public is another method of fund procurement. Emphasis is often placed on monthly guides which list the programs to be aired. These guides are mailed to a prepaid membership—usually at one dollar per month—or distributed free through various commercial outlets. Strategically located throughout the guide is a plea for financial support for the station's evening operation. Donations are requested for $10 family, $25 associate, $50 honor, or $100 institutional or executive memberships. Contributions to most stations are tax deductible. The administrator's responsibility in the overall production and distribution of program guides is minimal, but he must remain alert to possibilities of improving layout designs and increasing efficiency in the methods used by his station.

Procurement of operating funds through grants, private or governmental, usually stems from the imagination and creativeness of the station's staff. A recent development of the Blue Ridge ETV Association, Inc., might serve as an example. Forty hospitals are within the coverage area, and each hospital had undertaken to offer in-service training at an average annual cost of $1,000 per institution. This in-service training proved unsatisfactory; the response to classes was sporadic, and attendance ranged from two to twenty-five. Courses designed by all the institutions could be aired on WBRA-TV for approximately one-half the current cost per institution. The instruction could reach a much larger number of students, and the revenues of WBRA-TV would be increased by $20,000.

In recent years several educational television stations have undertaken on-the-air auctions. Station KQED, San Francisco, was the first station to launch such an effort, and has been most successful. To quote the adage "nothing succeeds like success" the educational television auction is now being used in Jacksonville, Florida (WJCT), in Boston (WGBH), and in Chicago (WTTW). Several other stations are contemplating auctions in the near future.

The successful station to some degree reflects the ability of the administrator to analyze the community and the capabilities of his station's facilities in the procurement of operational funds. Obviously, uniqueness of approach, diversity of methods used, and the multiplicity of efforts will determine the administrator's success in making his station financially stable.

Summary

Naturally, all the concepts contained in this chapter depend on a free exchange of ideas and information between the top management of an

CHAPTER 7

Evaluation of Learning From Televised Instruction

by

Keith W. Mielke

The purpose of this chapter is to give an overview of the problems of evaluating learning from televised instruction. It is not to be a summary of research findings nor a set of guidelines for conducting research, but a more general view of instructional television (ITV) research problems and contributions. Rather than considering the evaluation of learning as an "end of project" or "post-mortem" exercise I hope to show the relevance of the research function at all stages of the ITV process. The research specialist can be a valuable resource person as a member of the planning and execution team along with the teachers, administrators, curriculum consultants, and media specialists.

Defining Research

What is research? As an oversimplified statement, the research process (in ITV and elsewhere) consists of (1) defining terms, (2) asking questions or stating propositions which incorporate the defined terms in some explanatory fashion, and (3) seeking clear answers to the questions or unambiguous tests of the propositions. The first category is concerned with problems of measurement, conceptual clarity, and specifying objectives. The second category consists of analytical problems, understanding or explaining an expected concrete event in terms of more general principles or theories—putting structure on the problem. The third category deals with methodological problems, setting up conditions where observations can be interpreted as clear support or lack of support for the analytical-theoretical question. These definitions and divisions, although somewhat arbitrary in number and scope, will be useful in organizing the rest of the chapter.

From a subjective viewpoint, the scientific theory-research process as a way of grappling with ITV problems is more interesting than the presently available ITV research product. Much of the current research product lacks interest and/or utility because not enough effort was expended on the research categories one and two just described: defining terms and structuring the precise question to be asked. Although the third category of research methodology is extremely important, and many studies are uninterpretable because of faulty research designs, the major problem with the current body of ITV research literature is not the methodology for obtaining answers. The big problem is the poor, superficial, or absent rationales for asking the research questions.

Specifying Objectives

Along with any rational man, the ITV researcher strives for logical consistency and clear thought. Surely one of the least exotic demands of the ITV researcher is his insistence that tangible educational objectives be specified before research or evaluations are attempted. For most persons, this fundamental prerequisite to rational analysis is easy to accept intellectually, but more difficult to deliver. It is clear, however, that the concept of "evaluation" is meaningless in the absence of a specified goal. It should also be clear that the problem of specifying instructional objectives is not limited to ITV; it is a well-established educational problem whether the instruction is conveyed by television or any other medium.

It is easy enough to state objectives in vague form ("become a well-rounded individual," "achieve maximum potential," "develop an esthetic sense," "acquire habits of good citizenship"). The real problem lies in specifying objectives in behavioral terms. What should the learner be able to do? What exactly are you attempting to measure? What are the units or scales of measurement? What readings on the measuring instrument are to be called "success" and what shall be called "failure"? The researcher must ask these kinds of disturbing and difficult questions. Even if they cannot be answered with any degree of finality or certainty, it is better to grapple with the question and know that you are falling short of a satisfactory answer than to ignore the question.

Specifying objectives in behavioral terms is not merely an exercise for the benefit of the researcher; the teacher is the main beneficiary. If everyone who taught tried to specify his objectives in behavioral terms, it is likely that some would discover confusion on what their goals were. Others would see that their goals were quite unrealistic or that their greatest causes of concern were unrelated to their objectives.

It is especially difficult to specify learning objectives in behavioral terms for what is sometimes called affective learning, which concerns the realm of attitudes, opinions, and values. It is usually easier to specify cognitive (e.g., factual tests) or motor skill (e.g., typing speed-accuracy tests) types of objectives. The term "training" might fit comfortably in the area of cognitive or motor skill objectives. The term "education," however, has connotations for most people that extend into the affective realm. The science teacher not only wants his students to learn certain facts, he also wants them to develop their sense of curiosity. The music teacher wants the students to appreciate the music as well as to identify it. In political science or government, the teacher wants the students to develop a sense of excitement about the challenge of analyzing governments and working with them.

Affective learning objectives typically are either not stated at all, or else they are buried in "catalog rhetoric." They are rarely stated in behavioral terms because of their elusive nature. A classroom teacher, for example, may have a rather vague feeling or an untested conviction that his course has some effect on the attitudes of his students, but his measures for evaluation deal only with cognitive elements; for example, ability to supply correct answers to objective tests, ability to solve mathematical problems, ability to reproduce an experiment satisfactorily. When asked to consider teaching over television, this vague feeling emerges as a verbalized concern for perhaps the first time: "But if I go on TV, will the students get this or that value out of the course?" When asked how those values have been assessed in the past, he realizes that the measurement of affective learning has been most imprecise, if not nonexistent.

Measurement

Measurement of affective learning taxes the ingenuity. How, for instance, does a student who is excited and involved with the challenge and complexity of analyzing the operations of government differ, in measurable behavior, from a student who had mastered the same facts but is very unexcited about the whole area? There is no simple answer. The students can report that they have become excited about the study of government. Teachers or other observers can report that the students have become involved. Students can respond to various attitude scales designed to index this affective behavior. Various physiological measures (i.e., pupil dilation, galvanic skin response) are possible, but impractical outside the research laboratory. Various voluntary behaviors can be linked to affective learning such as voluntary extra reading, a choice of government as an academic major, a decision to pursue a career in government, a recommendation to a friend that he should take the course because it is interesting and exciting, and other behaviors of this nature. Each type of affective measure has its strengths and drawbacks, but none is as straightforward as measurement of information acquisition on an objective test.

When we attempted to evaluate affective instructional effects associated with a televised course in Introduction to American Government at Indiana University, several different types of the measures suggested above were used. The simplest of these was a series of open-end questions completed by the students—what was liked best and least, what stood out as the most noteworthy parts of the course, what suggestions for improvement could be offered. Teaching assistants in charge of discussion sections were asked how they thought the students had reacted. Attitude scales were administered at the beginning and end of the semester covering such concepts as "Your Professor," "Government as an Academic Major," "Instructional Television," and "Government Work as a Profession." A more indirect measure was yielded by a standard occupational prestige scale. We felt that one index of increased favorability toward the field of government might be an increase in the occupational prestige attributed to various roles in government. More out of curiosity than research imperative for this task, we administered items from an earlier Politico-Economic Conservatism scale to see if any measurable change in political ideology could be attributed to the course.

To the question, "Are we measuring the intangibles," Wilbur Schramm answers with unassailable logic: "The more 'intangible' they are, the less likely it is that they are being measured."[1] While no one would argue that the kinds of measures described above are ultimate indices of affective behavior, they do represent conscious attempts to make tangible a cluster of elusive instructional effects. The case for bringing all learning objectives out into the open is summarized nicely by Charles McIntyre:

> One may take exception to the stress upon *measurable* behavior on the ground that some content may be included which apparently does not result in measurable behavior. This is fair comment, but let him who so objects be reminded of the burden which is upon him of demonstrating that any learning has occurred if it cannot be measured.[2]

For instructional objectives, it is necessary to know and specify what you want to achieve before you can tell whether you have achieved it. This logical requirement for goal specification and measurement does not change as the objectives become less obvious or more impressionistic. If one were concerned with the evaluation of learning from televised instruction only in the sense of assessment against some standard, there would be no point in pursuing this topic further. For any given group of students, simply set the standard (specify the goal) and take a measure. Procedures for the evaluation of learning in some form or another were well established in the classroom long before the advent of ITV. The only apparent rationale for a special concern with evaluating learning from televised instruction is some suspicion, hunch, or rationale that the medium of television might affect learning in some manner. At this point, the concerns of category one—precise definitions of terms and behavioral specifications of objectives—are not sufficient by themselves to handle analytical questions such as media effects. What factors are relevant to the learning objectives? What factors are under the control of the teacher or the ITV producer? How does the medium of television interact with these factors? These questions demand that the problem be structured in a way that promotes analysis and understanding in addition to mere description. They are the concerns of category two in the research process—formulating good questions and propositions.

Formulating Research Questions and Propositions

Even at a primitive level, a suspicion that the medium of television might somehow affect learning is a step beyond the mere question of "what" to a faint recognition of the question of "why." That is, if students learn more or learn less from televised instruction than they do from "regular" instruction in the classroom, then, the argument continues, the differences should be attributable, for one reason or another, to the *medium* of television.

Why should television, per se, affect learning? The more organized and systematic the approach to this question, the more likely the approach will follow some implicit or explicit model of the instructional process, and the place of media within that process.

One simple and frequently cited model of communication was formulated by Harold Lasswell:

(1) Who

    (2) says what

        (3) through which channel

            (4) to whom

                (5) with what effect

In any communication situation, this model suggests, it would be useful in an analysis to consider the five kinds of factors listed above. Consider the Lasswell model as it would apply to the process of learning from televised instruction. The learning would come under the "effects" category. The "who" becomes the teacher; the "says what" becomes the content of the instruction; the "through which channel" becomes the medium or media of instruction; and the "to whom" becomes the students. When cast in the Lasswell model, the contributions of each of the first four categories—teacher, instructional content, and students, in addition to the *medium* of instruction—is relevant to the learning "effects." To analyze learning effects, the ITV researcher cannot restrict himself to media factors alone, but must try to account for all those factors that are highly related to learning.

The model contains no particular answers but it does help in asking a better question. The analytical framework provided by the model imposes a discipline on our thinking about ITV, a discipline which can make the difference between a useful research proposition and a trivial proposition. Why should students learn more or less from televised instruction than they do from instruction via any other medium?

The model suggests that a defensible proposition regarding the effects of a medium would also have to account for the variables associated with teachers, instructional content, and students.

In the general case, a factor would be considered relevant to learning with this analytical approach if, while holding the other three categories of factors constant or equivalent, changes in the fourth factor are associated with changes in effects (learning). For example, suppose teachers, content, and media are equivalent, but types of students differ (e.g., high and low aptitude). Three elements are held constant and the fourth element is varied. Given these conditions, the learning across the different types of students (high and low aptitude) would probably be different. This proposition sounds so reasonable that it probably sparks no research interest; that is, if a person knows what research question he is asking, it is unlikely that he would select this proposition as a research topic.[3] The only instances in which it might not hold true would be if the learning task were too difficult for either group or indiscriminately simple for both groups.

Consider another obvious example in which teachers, media, and students are equivalent, but the instructional content is varied. Matters which will not be included on the final examination are treated differently from those which will. There is little doubt that this instructional content factor is relevant to learning, and it is rarely questioned.

A less obvious question from the Lasswell model has generated more research in studies of persuasion and propaganda than in formal educational studies, though it does have implications for ITV. Given equivalent instructional content, media, and students, would different teachers elicit different degrees of learning? In general, there is more evidence that the "who" makes a difference in persuasive situations dealing with attitude change than in factual recall situations. Given a recognition of affective learning objectives, the "who" might be seen as a more relevant factor in ITV research as well.

Consider the medium now. Why should the medium of instruction affect learning? If teachers, instructional content, and students are held constant, is there any obvious change in expectations as the medium of instruction is varied from "live" settings to televised settings? When the question is forced into more precise statement, there is less basis for expecting television, per se, to have any effect whatsoever. In spite of it, the ITV research literature bulges with "TV versus face-to-face" comparisons of learning scores. We are dealing now with the theoretical question of why media differences should or should not be expected. In later paragraphs on methodology, it will be shown that many ITV research studies do not and/or cannot hold constant the teachers, the instructional content, and the students.

Media Effects

This example is provided to help consider the intuitive case for expecting no media differences: If you are in an airport reading the arrival and departure schedule from the bulletin board on the wall, are you not getting exactly the same information as a person reading the same schedule on a television screen in another part of the airport? Could the stimulus array from the actual bulletin board be expected to induce greater learning than the stimulus array on the closed-circuit television screen? Although one should maintain a critical attitude even toward things that appear to be patently obvious, it does seem that there are clear instances where the mediation of television makes no difference in learning effects, nor would such differences be reasonably expected. True, televising instruction is not the same as televising an airline schedule. The point here is that a good place to look for the meaningful relationships between instruction and media is in the examination of differences between (a) the clear case of no media effects (the airline schedule) and (b) the not-so-clear case of media effects (instruction).

Close examination of so-called media differences or effects discloses that many of these differences are not really characteristics of the media. In many cases, something which appears to be an inherent, defining characteristic of a medium, is at most a *typical correlate* of the medium. In other words, when televised instruction is compared with other modes of instruction, one of the problems is to determine what differences in learning are really due to television, and what differences are really due to other factors that have nothing to do, necessarily, with television.

Within the medium of television, there are qualities or characteristics which may be considered inherent. The stimulus array is small, two-dimensional, and for most current ITV, at least, monochromatic. Television utilizes two sensory modes: sight and sound. There is no allowance for audio or visual feedback unless special mediating hardware is provided. Given enough hardware, immediate, simultaneous, identical sight and sound messages can be made available to a theoretically limitless audience. Images can be recorded and replayed. Nearly any instructional resource or device that can be perceived in sight, sound, or motion can be presented on television. Within the limits of the system, images can be made larger or smaller. (The last three characteristics are, of course, shared with other media and devices.) This list of the inherent technical limitations and the inherent technical possibilities of the medium is probably incomplete, but it is sufficient to make the point. *Many of the actual criticisms of televised instruction do not deal with inherent or necessary limitations of television. Similarly, many of the praises are not directed to any unique quality of television, per se, but to praiseworthy practices available to several media.* The following is a concrete example of this point.

One of a series of open-end questions given to students taking the televised course in American Government at Indiana University asked specifically for criticisms. The major criticism concerned the discussion sessions, which were "live." The complaint against the inability to ask questions during lectures is relevant to the television medium, but not exclusively so. Criticisms of the textbook, the testing methods, and the time the class was offered are obviously not the unique domain of televised instruction. Students were also asked what they liked best. The four most frequently volunteered items were guest interviews, films, the lectures (interesting, tight organization), and the supplementary lesson outlines, none of which can be identified as inherent or unique to the medium of television.

The stimulus array for the "live" airlines schedule in the earlier example was equivalent to the stimulus array for the televised airline schedule. One can usually find differences between the stimulus arrays of televised instruction and its "live" counterpart. Many of these differences are not inherent in the media themselves, but are "optional" differences used to exploit the potentialities of one medium or another. Something is easy, compelling, or financially feasible to do with a medium, so it is done; and these things become associated with the medium itself. It is certainly possible to have well-organized lectures or lessons on television, or in an auditorium, or in the smallest of classes. Without being necessarily so, the degree of lesson organization may qualify as a typical correlate of the television medium in education. If televising means that instruction can now be witnessed and criticized by colleagues and others, if recording on video-tape means a long-term usage of the lesson, if expensive production procedures encourage greater preparation, if a supporting technical staff is available to prepare materials, if an absence of questions demands that the presentation have a logical progression of its own, then these factors can lead to more highly organized and better prepared lessons for televised instruction. *If the degree of lesson organization is relevant to learning, it should be properly labeled as lesson organization, not as an inherent quality of the television medium.*

If media, per se, elicit favorable or unfavorable attitudes, and if, in turn, these attitudes affect learning, then media, per se, can be said to affect learning from yet another perspective, independent of the stimulus array. Once again, precise thinking will separate the correlates of attitude favorability into (a) inherent media characteristics and (b) typical practices associated, but not necessarily identified, with the media. If students detest any monochromatic two-dimensional stimulus array, then televised instruction is in some difficulty. However, if the student is unfavorable toward ITV because he feels "depersonalized," that no one is concerned with him as an individual, then it should be useful to separate this source of unfavorability from television. Impersonality, not television, would be the analytic clue to understanding the unfavorable attitude.

Impersonality is not always present with televised instruction and it is not always absent from "live" instruction. Classifying instruction into categories of media is not the way to come to grips with the problem of impersonality in instruction. The point is illustrated by two pilot surveys conducted when the freshman course in Government referred to above was in the process of being recorded on video-tape. Students in both pilot surveys responded on a seven-point scale to this question: "In general, how personally involved or detached have you felt in the average lecture?" In one survey period, the professor left the campus for a period of time. His lectures were replaced by prerecorded lessons he had prepared, and discussion sections were conducted by his graduate assistant. In the second survey period, nearly all of the course consisted of the newly recorded televised lessons, but the professor himself conducted his own discussion sessions. On the seven-point scale, with seven representing maximum personal involvement, the first survey averaged 3.9, but the second survey averaged 5.2. The students in the second pilot survey did not feel depersonalized during televised lectures because they had ready access to the professor during discussion sessions. In fact, respondents in the second survey preferred the televised lectures supplemented by the professor leading his own "live" discussion over total live instruction by the same professor. The combination gave them the best of both methods. If this interpretation of the data is valid, it may suggest ways to increase, rather than decrease, the amount of personal contact with students through the use of televised instruction. More relevant to the present argument, however, is the analytic separation of media and impersonality. With the factor "degree of impersonality," one may assess any instruction—live, televised, computerized, filmed, or whatever. If that factor is highly relevant to the evaluation of learning, it clouds the issue to identify it solely with the medium of instruction.

Asking an imprecise question often leads to uninterpretable or misleading results. The gross and unelaborated "TV versus face-to-face" category of study typifies the problems inherent in an imprecise question. The typical finding in these comparisons is "no significant difference" or NSD. Finding NSD is somewhat analogous to discovering NSD in learning between blonds and brunettes. One might say that blonds are "as good as" brunettes in terms of learning. But, more to the point, one would also have to say that knowledge of hair color is of no help in predicting, controlling or understanding learning; that is, there is no reliable relationship between the factor "hair color" and the factor "amount of learning." The ITV researcher, however, is trying to establish stable relationships among relevant factors, not a lack of relationships. The proposition "Learning under conditions of X is greater than learning under conditions of Y" states a positive relationship. It suggests that the instructor should maximize the quality X, thereby increasing the amount of learning. What does the NSD finding suggest? To the extent that one would have no good reason for expecting a difference in learning between blonds and brunettes (or TV versus face-to-face), or to the extent that one could not explain the difference if he did find it, it was a bad question to ask in the first place, from a theoretic point of view.

Essentially, the argument up to this point has been a plea for specifying in behavioral terms both cognitive and affective learning objectives, accounting for the nature of the medium of television in terms of its effect on the stimulus material, analytically separating factors that are media characteristics from factors that have been called media correlates, and relating these more precise analyses to general multivariate theories of communication and learning. This particular section has dealt with some problems of asking good questions relevant to learning from televised instruction.

The quality of an answer can rarely rise above the quality of the question. Given a good question, the quality of an answer then depends on methodological soundness.

Methodology

It would be desirable to test and verify such statements as, "Learning under conditions of X will be greater than learning under conditions of Y." Rather than dealing with the logical and theoretical bases for making (or avoiding) such statements, this section deals briefly with some of the major methodological problems in answering questions or testing theoretic propositions in the ITV area. The job of the methodologist is to see if X and Y are actually related to increments in learning, and in so doing, to minimize, control, or otherwise account for any factors other than X and Y which might be influencing learning. The problem with a "feeling" that something hinders or enhances learning is the subjective and nonsystematic nature by which the supporting data are gathered. Both advocates and critics of ITV have on occasion exhibited this rather human weakness. The methodologist is supposed to discipline relevant data so the evidence answers the intended question and no other.

Two basic criteria for good questions are: Is the question analytically sound (theoretic relevance, logical consistency, precise definition of terms, appropriate labels)? Is the question answerable (capable of being made tangible for controlled observation)? The question "Which leads to greater learning, televised or live instruction?" not only has the theoretical problems discussed earlier; such a question also introduces severe methodological problems. It is very difficult to conduct an investigation in the "TV versus face-to-face" context that is both highly controlled and meaningful. If in the transition from live to televised instruction, the teacher changes, the scheduling changes, the teaching aids change, the type or amount of lesson preparation changes, the size or composition of the class changes, was it these changes or the change of medium (or both) that accounted for any observed differences in learning? The kind of nonmedium changes mentioned here tend to occur, and they tend to influence experimental measures, such as learning. Without methodological controls, one may in fact be answering such irrelevant (to this chapter) questions as: Who learns more, students taught by an organized teacher or a disorganized teacher? Who learns more, bright students or dull students?

Realizing the pitfalls of reaching conclusions from an uncontrolled investigation, a researcher might do in fact what was earlier considered hypothetically with the propositions from the Lasswell model: equate two instructional groups on everything except the instructional medium. Such a study might place a camera in the back of a live classroom; then whatever the teacher did with the students in the room would supposedly be transmitted to another group of similar students in a TV receiving room. This method seems, on the surface, to be methodologically "tight." In a sense, however, the investigator is damned if he doesn't control and damned if he does in the "TV versus face-to-face" context. That is, the greater the forced adherence of televised instruction to the patterns and procedures of regular classroom instruction, the fewer positive things one can do to exploit that which television is well equipped to do. The question being asked may be this: In which situation is there greater learning—optimized live instruction or handicapped televised instruction?

The televised course in Government at Indiana University contained interviews with various persons of national prominence, who were on campus for one reason or another. The interviews were scheduled at their convenience, recorded on video-tape, and subsequently integrated into the appropriate part of the course. One of the instructional potentials of the television medium was put to good use. It was not a necessary or inherent quality of the medium; it was one of those "may or may not do" qualities that distinguish between using the medium and merely "plugging it in." The classes receiving live instruction had no opportunity to witness the interviews, hence the dilemma. Did the medium of television make any difference, or did the different content made available by television make a difference? From the point of view of experimental controls, the inclusion of guest interviews was an added ambiguity in the process of interpreting the comparative effects of the course. From the point of view of good instruction, however, it would have been incongruous not to do the best job possible with the televised instruction.

When compared to the difficulty of asking good questions, the problem of methodology is simple. Yet those who critically review the literature of ITV regularly charge methodological inadequacy. David W. Stickell has argued cogently that the findings of ITV research summarized in review articles should be qualified by the adequacy of the methodology that generated the finding; for example, two findings, one with sound methodology and the other with bad methodology, should not be given equal credibility in a review of the literature. Stickell systematically analyzed 250 "TV versus face-to-face" comparisons on methodological criteria with devastating results: Only 10 of the 250 comparisons were classified as "interpretable"; 23 were classified as "partially interpretable"; the remaining 217 were classified as "uninterpretable."[4]

Tight methodology in ITV research is difficult enough even under ideal conditions. Almost any research design contains compromises from the ideal, especially when the research must be conducted within a structure that does not have research as one of its goals. That is one reason the research specialist should be consulted earlier rather than later in an ITV project. The more demanding the methodology required by a particular research question, the more difficult it is to conduct the investigation with regularly scheduled classes. Demands of research, such as randomly assigned students, lengthy testing periods, and tight control over content, can quickly come into conflict with the instructional demands. The amount of control given the researcher can determine whether he is able to conduct formal research or simply make an evaluation.

An evaluation is considered here as an extension of or a supplement to the regular evaluative measures taken during a course. It would not have as its goal the rigorous testing of hypotheses or contributions to theory any more than a store taking inventory intends to contribute something to economic theory. An evaluation would describe, but not explain; it would enumerate effects, but would not specify causes. Under this definition, much of the literature on instructional television would be classified as evaluations rather than research projects. There will always be a need for evaluations, but they should not be asked to transcend their methodological limitations inherent in most ongoing formal classes. Evaluations can take inventory and even suggest hypotheses, but they should not be offered as proof of hypotheses. Formal research projects, on the other hand, would be designed to test hypotheses. Whether conducted in the research laboratory or with ongoing classes, the researcher would have a tight design and sufficient control over events to implement that design.

Rigorous methodology cannot turn a bad question into a good one. Nonrigorous methodology can, however, prevent a good question from being answered. The researcher's request of the teacher or administrator for special consideration to make a study more rigorous should be viewed in that light. If an ITV research project is worth doing at all, it is worth doing well.

Observations and Opinions

No amount of research can specify what the learning objectives should be, and research cannot measure metaphysical learning objectives. Once the behavioral objectives have been decided, the researcher can be put to good use. The theory-research man comes to the instructor or the administrator with two things in his tool kit: some general principles of communication and learning, and some methodological-analytical skills. With the theories, models, and conceptual schema, he can probe for certain kinds of statements, but he cannot supply the specific statement of objectives. Given a statement of objectives, he can suggest methods for reaching the objectives. Given a statement of behavioral objectives, a researcher can state whether these objectives are being achieved, or to what extent they are not being achieved. Given two or more methods for achieving behavioral learning objectives, the researcher can determine the relative efficiency of the alternatives. The research person should be able to give assistance and suggestions on the measurement of difficult-to-measure objectives. Given an instructional message with unknown effects, a research person can, to some extent, find out what the effects are.

The research person can be a source of feedback to the instructor with supplementary information. For example, the researcher, as part of his design for control and precision, might stratify students on such variables as ability levels. Secondary findings of considerable interest can emerge this way; for example, that version A of a presentation is more successful for high IQ students, but version B is better for low IQ students. The instructor, on his own, would not normally gather such cross-tabulations.

With his knowledge of the research literature, the researcher can serve as a resource person. While the research literature in ITV is not outstanding from a theoretical or methodological point of view, many studies report instructional techniques that could be interesting and helpful to an instructor or administrator. Especially when going into televised instruction for the first time, even the "Here is how we did it in Podunk" kind of reports can be useful.

The researcher can frequently be of as much assistance in the questions he asks as in the answers he supplies. With an empirical and analytical approach, he can help expose poor questions before they are translated into poor practices. The research function can be much more successfully used if there is a prior understanding of what it can and cannot be expected to do.

The research literature in ITV is far too extensive for any summary to be attempted here.[5] Some of the general characteristics should be examined, however, because nearly every researcher who has conducted a critical and extensive literature review has been pessimistic. Several reasons for this point of view have been mentioned earlier, but there are a few others. There is no systematic method of classification in the field of instructional TV. Hundreds of variables enter into the instructional television process, and these variables are not systematically related under any unified scheme. Consider the problem: Should subject matter form a category? Grade level? Methodology? Theoretic orientation, if any? Type of transmission? Hypotheses tested, if any? Control variables? The list can go on and on, with concomitant increments of frustration. Without some unifying theoretic concepts, it is difficult to say whether experiment A tests something essentially different from experiment B.

A subsidiary problem to the problem of classification is the lack of uniform definitions. What does "learning" mean? In one study it means typing speed; in another it means the judged quality of an essay for a college English class; in another it means the score on Miss Jones's final examination in ninth grade algebra. What does "regular instruction" mean when comparisons are made with regular instruction? What do "highly visualized" and "feedback" mean? Either a new research with greater precision is called for, or at least some conventions are needed.

There are no uniform standards of reporting. Ideally, a research report should specify procedures in such a way that other scholars could repeat the study. With the lack of a workable classification system and a lack of uniform definitions, however, research reports in ITV tend to give scanty information. Reports of government-sponsored research in ITV, such as the NDEA Title VII Projects, tend to be better in this regard.

There is a general lack of theoretic relevance. To say it another way, many studies were initiated as descriptive evaluations with no carefully considered expectations to test empirically.

There are apparent contradictions in the research findings. The word "apparent" is used because of a faith that no "true" contradictions exist. There are critically different populations studied and controls exerted. There are different definitions of terms and different idiosyncracies of the moment, but there are no true contradictions. It is strongly felt that as soon as researchers can agree on the nature of the phenomena being studied, the number of apparent contradictions will show a significant decrease.

It can be seen that all these problems are related. The definitional problem leads to the problem of contradictions and contributes to the problem of classification. All relate to the theoretical problem. It is perhaps of some comfort to say that ITV is by no means alone with this set of problems, that these problems are now widely recognized, and that the level of sophistication of both questions and methodology in ITV is increasing noticeably.

In conclusion, the problem of evaluating learning from televised instruction is not a simple one, especially if the evaluation is supposed to contribute something to understanding and controlling the learning process, as opposed to merely describing some of its more apparent characteristics. While television in education has brought into being several new professional roles, it is not at all clear that television has staked out for itself a new theory of instruction. There is even less reason to believe that general principles of human behavior were somehow different after the arrival of television. Fundamental questions that were relevant to learning before television are still relevant: How is meaning translated into symbolic form by one person and decoded by another person? What is the nature of a medium? How do people learn? The strategy of relating the specific characteristics of the television medium to more general models of communication and learning suggests that many of the pertinent issues are not television issues at all, but are general issues in learning and communication.

CHAPTER 8

Some Questions about Instructional Television

by

RICHARD BURKE

THERE IS A TEMPTATION to conclude a book about an aspect of education with a chapter entitled "The Outlook for the Future" or "Tomorrow's Instructional Technology," or a title which describes institutions and environments that are an ideal blend of scientific method, application of technology, and humanistic concern for the well-being of the individual. This type of prognostication, however, usually fails to take into account the process of change and the evolution of new forms and practices. Johnny Brooke, whose school day was described in the Introduction, may be a typical beneficiary of advanced educational technology and advanced thinking in the behavioral sciences, but it is difficult to see or imagine the various stages of progress and change that education went through in order to arrive at such a sophisticated finished product. Furthermore, all students will not be learning under the same conditions as Johnny Brooke, any more than all students are learning under the same conditions at the present time. There will be a wide range of possibilities and alternatives, and any single model of the future tends to be too selective in presenting only one configuration of a learning environment.

In this final chapter, I hope to suggest some lines of inquiry which may prove useful in the future of television and education. Questions must be asked, remote possibilities explored, and old assumptions challenged, if we are to take the first steps toward discovering new relationships between television and the process of learning.

The authors of this book have discussed various patterns of use for television in education. It has been suggested, for instance, that television can make a valuable contribution to education by bringing to the student live coverage of events, such as space shots, special meetings of the United Nations, or the proceedings of governmental bodies at the state and local levels. There really is not much argument about using television in this way, because teachers and administrators generally feel that there is value in allowing students to see such events as they take place. There may be some disagreement over which events are worth viewing in their entirety, which deserve limited attention, and which could just as well be missed; but these are minor differences of opinion, since these televised happenings occupy a very small percentage of total instructional time.

Another pattern of use for television has been as a curriculum enrichment device. In this context, the teacher uses television on a more or less regular basis to enrich the learning experiences of the students. The teacher may ask the class to view certain programs on commercial or educational television as part of regular homework assignments. He may be using these programs to provide information, to provoke classroom discussion, or simply because he feels that the students would benefit from watching an artistic performance or a series of public affairs programs. If the teacher wants to make assignments of this nature and the students have access to television receivers, there is no reason why he should not make use of such programs in his teaching. Television may also be used as an enrichment device during the regular school day. Many stations provide programs which are designed to add enrichment and information to education, and if the teacher can fit them into the schedule, he is allowed to use them if he wishes. The general feeling among educators seems to be that television as curriculum enrichment is related to films, assembly programs, field trips, or guest speakers in the classroom. The television programs provide a break in the routine and experiences that otherwise might not be available; they are allowed as long as they do not seriously disrupt the day-to-day business of teaching and learning.

In both instances—television as an occasional experience or as a curriculum enrichment device—a context of use is assumed in which a teacher in charge of a certain number of students in a defined environment has the power to exercise control over the quality and quantity of televised experiences. The factor of control is vital to the formal relationship between the teacher and the taught. The experience of television is perceived as incidental, permissible if nondisruptive, and peripheral to the learning process. Is this traditional relationship as secure as it appears? In thinking that control over the influence of television in the formal learning situation is really significant, have we missed the point?

John I. Goodlad, Dean of the Graduate School of Education at U.C.L.A., emphasized the impact of other influences on the student in a speech on the future of learning and teaching:

> The average high school senior graduating this past June has viewed 15,000 hours of television in addition to many hundreds of hours of public movies. These hours and many more spent with newspapers and magazines exposed him to a formidable display of violence, cruelty, dishonesty, and inhumanity to man. I do not believe that his 12,000 hours in school exposed him to anything like an antidote. And school intensity throughout was low. We appear loath to portray the other side of the coin through the substance of schooling. Could we not mount a program in the social studies and in the humanities designed to portray the best in men and in mankind? We have the tools and the creative minds. Do we not care enough, or have we simply resigned ourselves to inevitable folly in man?[1]

"The new learner is the result of the new media," said Father John Culkin, communications expert at Fordham University, "and a new learner calls for a new kind of learning."[2] Are we adapting the process of learning to accommodate the child who comes to school with a vast reservoir of vicarious experiences, who is accustomed to communication through image and sound, and who wants to use all of his senses in his learning as an active agent in the process of discovery?

Formal Instruction by Television

Although most educators cautiously agree that television may contribute to learning as a cultural enrichment device, they seem to have many reservations about televised instruction as an integral part of the learning experience. The authors of this book have made a strong case for the adoption of instructional television into our educational system, but advocacy and enthusiasm are not sufficient guarantees of success. According to the Carnegie Commission's massive study of public television: "Instructional television, like instructional radio and instructional motion pictures before it, lies outside the process, put to incidental or occasional use as ancillary material. With minor exceptions, the total disappearance of instructional television would leave the educational system fundamentally unchanged."[3]

The commission's point of view is strongly supported by Judith Murphy and Ronald Gross:

> Whether measured by the numbers of students affected, or by the quality of the product, or by the advancement of learning, televised teaching is still in a rudimentary stage of development. The medium can take credit for helping understaffed schools to cope with ever increasing enrollments. But television has not transformed education nor has it significantly improved the learning of most students. In short, TV is still far from fulfilling its obvious promise. Television is *in* education all right, but it is still not *of* education.[4]

Gross and Murphy believe that instructional television's limited influence can be largely explained by a deficiency in quality.

The Quality of Televised Instruction

A deficiency in quality may mean that the production values in a particular program are weak; camera work is poorly conceived; videotape quality is unsatisfactory; or lighting, design, and graphics are poorly executed. More often, however, it means that a program is unsuitable because it is not very effective instruction: the content may be out of date, poorly structured, or uninteresting; the teacher may be dull, uninformed, or disorganized and fail to stimulate the learner. A single overwhelming factor or a combination of factors may cause a program to be labeled deficient in quality.

If poor quality is a major cause of disenchantment or indifference, it is tempting for the instructional television specialist to absolve himself by saying that the quality of instruction is not a television problem but, rather, an instructional problem. To some extent such a view is justified, and the Carnegie Commission emphasized this point:

> One accomplishment of instructional television, desirable if it stimulates appropriate action, has been to make evident shortcomings in the training and the support of teachers, clearly

permeating the entire public educational system. Teachers who appear on television are usually men and women devoted to their calling, and responsive to their pupils; yet they must frequently struggle with a badly prepared syllabus and textbook, and without the variety of teaching aids, new and old, which a vigorous educational system might easily provide for them. It is not so much the deficiencies of instructional television that are laid bare, but the deficiencies of public education itself.[5]

The instructional television producer can adopt the attitude that he is a specialist in communications, and if the content or the teaching methodology is inadequate, there is nothing he can or should do about it. This kind of fragmentary thinking persists, but fortunately more and more practitioners are beginning to see how pointless and unproductive it has been. The best approach to quality in instructional television is a team approach, which is neither teacher oriented nor media oriented, but learner oriented. The teacher, the curriculum specialist, the learning theorist, and the media specialist must attempt to design learning experiences that are free from the traditional restraints of course outlines, textbooks, and the conventional teacher-learner relationship. In hundreds of instances, television courses have been developed and introduced into classrooms without the slightest re-examination of goals, objectives, and the means of achieving them. It was simply assumed that the teachers and the students would get more out of the course if it were on television, and this assumption was rarely examined in any detail.

A Systematic Approach to Planning

In the 1960's the concepts of "Systems analysis" or "instructional systems design" became prominent in the literature of educational planning. Borrowing from the systems concepts in biology, engineering, and psychology, educational planners have been applying some of them to education. A systems planner takes into account specified, measurable behavioral objectives; various strategies for attaining the objectives; devices for measuring the outputs of the system with respect to the objectives; and methods of ensuring feedback in the system.

"Generally," said C. R. Carpenter, "there has been oversimplification of the concept to the point where heterogeneous assemblies of media have been described as systems. More correctly, a system includes all of those components, elements, factors, operations, and conditions which are significantly related to the results and objectives of a defined educational effort. The people parts of a system are often the most important determinants of the system's level of performance."[6]

Instructional television can contribute very little to the learning process if it is superimposed on a rigid structure. Over and over again, it has been used as a device which adds something to a course of study, and it is little wonder that teachers have been, and continue to be, disenchanted with television. The question is not how and where do we fit television into the course of study; but, rather, we should be asking how will the learner achieve maximum learning; what resources are available; how should the learner be directed to various learning opportunities; what is the proper relationship between the teacher and the learner, the learner and other sources of information and stimulation; and how shall the desired objectives be measured?

The Carnegie Commission report pointed out that television has frequently made evident the shortcomings of teachers by exposing them to the scrutiny of their peers, their supervisors, and the public. Television may perhaps make one of its strongest contributions to education, if educators, when they think about integrating it into an educational system, are forced to define their goals more clearly, to assess the validity of some of the assumptions that they have been holding without examination, and to deal with the learning process in a more rational and meaningful way.

Some promising approaches to instructional planning are being pursued by National Instructional Television (formerly National Center for School and College Television) in Bloomington, Indiana. In addition to its functions as a national distribution center, NIT has assumed a strong role in the field of program design and development.

The NIT strategy has been to assess educational needs in certain curriculum areas, evaluate current offerings of existing program material, and design programs based on stated curriculum objectives. According to Edwin G. Cohen, executive director of NIT, "New production patterns will include a conceptual phase that uses the nation's most knowledgeable educators, rigorous specification of educational goals, identification of an effective television teacher, experimental development of presentation formats, testing and selection of the most promising format, perfection of a chosen format for pilot production and testing of lessons, tentative production and testing of additional lessons, revisions, further testing of production, broadcast, classroom feedback, revision, and general feedback."[7] If Mr. Cohen's predictions turn out to be accurate, production periods for new materials may cover several years.

Another promising development is the trend to cooperative production. For instance, a consortium of thirteen organizations cooperated with NIT to produce a series of programs on early childhood development. Besides greater input of ideas in the development stage, the consortium approach also provides a broader financial base to meet the costs of production in instructional television. If the consortium idea prevails, it should help to eliminate much of the current duplication of programs, since each station, school district, or state does essentially the same kind in its area.

Some Questions about Teaching and Presentation

Theoretically, the television teacher has more expertise in the subject matter, more assistance from professional communicators, and more time for research and preparation than the average classroom teacher. The television teacher, therefore, can present more material in a more exciting manner in less time than the classroom teacher. If this argument is valid and the television teacher actually does have all these resources at his disposal, then, we are only dressing up and speeding up a method of instruction that may already be outmoded. If, as mentioned earlier in the chapter, the child of the media age comes to school accustomed to communication through sight and sound, ready to use all of his senses, why are we encouraging a method of instruction which is often irrelevant and inefficient? Probably the best answer is that many generations of students have been taught by the lecture-demonstration method, and we accept presentation and the presence of a talking teacher as synonymous with teaching.

Perhaps many television programs could be done more efficiently without the actual visual presence of a television teacher. Perhaps television should be used to present *only* those things that ordinarily would be unavailable to a classroom teacher, such as interviews with public figures; expensive, difficult or dangerous science experiments; or programs which take advantage of the electronic phenomena of television.

THE VISUAL MEDIUM

Because of its visual impact, television has been proposed as a powerful teaching device to reach the student who loses interest in school because his reading ability is inadequate or practically non-existent. It is entirely possible that television can make a contribution to the education of the poor reader, but television will not solve the problem without major changes of procedure and in the allocation of educational resources. We do not know if the nonreader is discouraged only because he cannot read, or because the whole situation in the classroom seems irrelevant and a waste of time. Television may retain the poor reader's interest for a time, but eventually someone will have to deal with the real problems of motivation and relevance. Unless the change of medium is accompanied by a change of message, we are deluding ourselves by expecting too much from the visual medium of television.

We may also be overestimating the ease with which material can be learned by means of television. If the image is nothing more than a talking teacher, comprehension probably does not present any problem, but what about more sophisticated uses of the visual medium? Is it necessary to learn how to "read" a nonprint means of communication? Is there, for instance, a language or grammar of visual communication which must be mastered in order to be truly fluent in using and responding to the medium? Many theorists on visual perception feel that there is a language and grammar of film and television, and that we have not yet grasped the structure and techniques of visual communication. When we come closer to defining the nature of television, we shall perhaps see more clearly how to use television in the classroom.

Television and the Education of Teachers

STUDENT TEACHERS

Television is being used more and more to facilitate student teacher observation of classroom practices. Since the traditional methods of observation frequently result in wasted travel time, crowded conditions in the classroom, and considerable annoyance and disruption to the teacher and students being observed, several universities have installed television systems that link laboratory schools or cooperating elementary and secondary schools and the School or Department of Education on campus. Teachers in training can observe classrooms on television monitors in special viewing rooms; and if the system includes a video-tape recorder, it is possible to see certain practices over and over again, stop the recording to repeat a particular section, or simply to preserve examples of outstanding teaching.

At one university, which has a large number of students in special education, television is used to provide visual case studies for teachers and counselors. A child with a severe speech difficulty, for instance, might be brought to the clinic at age three, and his therapy sessions might go on for five or six years. Taped transcripts of all the sessions can be made with television camera and video-tape recorder. Shortened or edited versions can then be made for the teacher in training, so that a student teacher or therapist can see and hear the child's stages of development on video-tape in as much detail as is necessary.

Another important use of television in teacher training is the method of presentation, observation, and criticism known as "micro-teaching." There are any number of refinements in micro-teaching, but basically the student teacher presents a limited amount of material to a small group of listeners, while a television camera records the student teacher's presentation. After the material has been presented, and the students are given a chance to respond to the presentation, the video-tape is played back to the student teacher and his critic teacher. On the basis of student comments and questions, the observations and critical comments of the supervising teacher, and self-observation, the student teacher is given another opportunity to repeat the same unit of material to the same group of listeners. How many times this process takes place is left to the discretion of the supervising critic teacher, but the process of immediate evaluation, feedback, and self-appraisal has obvious advantages in the preparation of student teachers. It is not a particularly expensive method of teacher training, nor does it require a great deal of modification in classroom environments. It does require a certain amount of time to bring about the desired results, and it takes an experienced and thoughtful critic teacher to make the micro-teaching pay off in true benefit to the student.

When a student teacher becomes acquainted with instructional television through classroom observation, micro-teaching, or some other application, he should be more willing to accept the idea that learning can take place in a variety of ways, with a variety of methods. He may also see that television can play an important part in the total learning experience and take the first steps toward becoming a manager of learning situations.

IN-SERVICE EDUCATION FOR TEACHERS
AND SUPERVISORY PERSONNEL

The literature of instructional television is filled with suggestions for its use in the continuing education of teachers and supervisory personnel. Television can be used to present demonstrations, model classes, presentations by special guests, orientation sessions, and any other information which must be made available to teachers and supervisors on a continuing basis.

Suppose, for example, that every elementary teacher in New York City has to see a discussion-demonstration on new techniques in the teaching of reading. Giving it several times and perhaps in several places is cumbersome, time-wasting, and expensive. On television it could be presented once or twice at a convenient hour, perhaps 4:00 P.M., and a large majority of the teachers in the city, or for that matter in the entire state, could see the program at the same time. Quite often, questions can be telephoned in to the television studio at the time of the demonstration, or a follow-up program can be given a week later, after the teachers have tried out a few suggestions with their own classes.

Supervisors, principals, and other administrative personnel could learn a great deal from each other by participating in a tele-conference every month, or every two months, on a city or state-wide basis. New teachers, especially in a large city system, could be given the usual pre-Labor Day orientation on television, with a subsequent follow-up at their schools.

Comments by interviewees in a study made by the Fund for Media Research indicated considerable satisfaction with school television:

> The most successful use of television here has been the Superintendent's presentation of the Board Report. It was a high quality program. The teachers of the community enjoy getting the information at the same time.

TV beamed into school is great in overcoming the decline of teacher's institutes (as mandated by the unions), meeting needs in areas where teachers feel insecure, like the New Math, Linguistics, mass media, and Social Studies.

The lack of communication in a system as large as ours and a lack of knowledge of what is going on are tremendous. The teachers simply don't know. The teachers' organizations are worse. Use of television by the Superintendent helps to give true, living perspective. He not only tells them what the policies are, but also conveys who is ultimately responsible for them. Bulletins are not enough. Closed-circuit television would help a great deal in getting much more of this.[8]

The study also noted that school television in the great cities had four major uses: instruction (90%); teacher education (5.6%); community information (2.9%); and administrative (1.2%). School systems in our large cities have not yet fully explored the potential of television for solving some of their problems in the distribution and sharing of personnel and instructional resources. The cities that use television are enthusiastic about it, and perhaps in the next few years we may see more activity in this particular application of television.

Other Uses of Television in Education

ADULT EDUCATION

In our preoccupation with instructional television, we have all too often failed to give attention to the potential of television to educate as well as entertain adults. Adult education, in fact, has been the forgotten area of Educational Television programming. When we realize that 62 million (more than 50 percent) of the adults of our nation have not graduated from high school, that 44 million have not completed the ninth grade, and that 2 million more have never gone to school at all, we can see the challenge which television offers for the continuing education of our citizens.[9]

Traditionally, we have thought of adult education as an activity that takes place in the local high school at night, in formally scheduled classes or meetings. The participants in these programs may be learning skills to enrich their leisure time, working toward college credits, or winding up the course work for a high school diploma. This kind of adult education is a perfectly legitimate enterprise, but its effect, as the above figures show, has been negligible in the context of mass education.

A number of institutions have offered courses for credit on television for persons unable to attend conventional on-site classes; but to make a significant change in the behavior of millions of adult learners, we need more offerings on a less formal and less structured basis. We have just begun to appreciate the distinctions between "education" and "schooling," and we must pursue this line of inquiry even further in our educational planning. For instance, if courses, credits, and formal classroom environments created frustration and hostility in many of the young adults who stopped going to school, perhaps schooling is not only inefficient but counter-productive to education. If television can serve as the catalyst to promote innovation and exploration in adult education, it will perform an extremely valuable service.

Television and the Preschool Child

We are just beginning to realize how much a child learns in his first five years and how many opportunities we have to provide worthwhile learning experiences for him. Researchers have discovered that preschoolers spend much time in front of their television sets, and we have been guilty of abandoning them to the cartoon shows and to other programs of questionable value to their learning process. A start has been made with programs like "Roundabout," "Mr. Rogers' Neighborhood," "Sesame Street," and "Ripples" but it is too early to tell which techniques of programming and production will best serve their needs. Television should make a strong contribution in the next few years to this vitally important area of human development.

Methods of Transmission and Distribution

The Educational Television Station

At the present time there are almost 200 educational television stations on the air. Some of them are licensed to colleges or universities; others are licensed to boards of education, school districts, or some other formal organization within the structure of public education; and the remainder are licensed to community organizations of one kind or another. Many educational television stations broadcast in-school material, pre-school material, programs for in-service teacher training, and adult education. The revenue derived from in-school broadcasting is a substantial part of their operating income.

A major advantage of broadcast television is that programs can be seen by anyone within reach of the station's broadcast signal. A viewer may be in a school room, at home, in a hospital, a church, or community organization. In other words, if the desired goal is to reach as many people as possible with television programs, open-circuit broadcast television would probably be the most desirable means of transmission.

One disadvantage of broadcast television, however, is the cost and complexity of the operation. It simply costs more to build and operate a television station than it does to run a closed-circuit operation, and the personnel requirements are more demanding, especially in the engineering and technical departments. The inflexibility in program scheduling is another disadvantage, which stations have attempted to overcome by scheduling the same program at different times on different days throughout the week. At a time when flexible scheduling is being used in so many schools, it is doubtful whether a significant number of them in any given area would adhere to rigid class schedules merely to take advantage of broadcast television programs.

CLOSED-CIRCUIT TELEVISION

Just as the name implies, closed-circuit television is "closed" in the sense that only a specified audience can view the programs, which are sent directly to receivers in the classrooms from a studio or video-tape recorder by means of a cable or microwave link. A closed-circuit system may mean a single television camera sending sound and picture to one or more receivers, or it may mean a highly sophisticated installation containing several cameras, a film chain, a switching device, and all the necessary accessories for a complex studio operation. A closed-circuit television installation can operate in only one school, and it can cover an entire county, as in Washington County, Maryland, or an entire state. Regardless of the physical area covered, only those schools or buildings that are directly connected to the studio or video-tape recorder can receive the programs. Unless they are part of the closed-circuit loop, sets in ordinary homes are unable to receive them. Although the recent expansion of cable television makes it possible for more people to subscribe to closed-circuit television in their homes, television for instructional purposes has not been used extensively in its programming.

Several advantages of closed-circuit television make it worth considering for instructional purposes:

1. Several courses can be televised at the same time on a closed-circuit system, and the individual student or the classroom teacher merely has to select the appropriate channel. With three or four channels operating simultaneously, many of the scheduling problems are modified or eliminated entirely.

2. Closed-circuit television gives a school or school district more control over interpretation of curriculum, teaching methodology, and media utilization. If a school district wishes to tailor a curriculum to meet its own educational needs, closed-circuit television provides more opportunity for close cooperation among curriculum designers, television teachers and producers, and classroom teachers.

3. Closed-circuit television facilities may be used in a large variety of programs, such as guidance and counseling, homeroom, school information, and any other activities which call for the resources of a sound and picture distribution system.

Despite these advantages, some educators feel that closed-circuit television tends to reinforce existing practices, rather than to stimulate change by providing models of excellence in curriculum, teaching methodology, and television production. They also know that it becomes prohibitively expensive, as the area to be covered increases in size. For certain geographic areas, especially those with high-density population, the ideal method of transmission would fall somewhere between closed-circuit and broadcast television. Perhaps the relatively new Instructional Television Fixed Service (also known as the 2500 megacycle band or, more properly, the 2500 megahertz band) may be the most practical compromise between the two systems.

Instructional Television Fixed Service

When the Federal Communications Commission established the Instructional Television Fixed Service in 1963 for use as an instructional medium, it said, "The primary purpose of the new service is to send visual and accompanying aural instructional material to selected receiving locations in public and private schools, colleges and universities, and other instructional centers for the formal education of students." Up to five programs may be transmitted and received simultaneously in any given educational institution. The 2500 MhZ system offers the multichannel flexibility of closed-circuit television, but the costs of installation are considerably lower, especially if the distances to be covered are from 15 to 20 miles. "Of special significance to administrators," explained the Commission, "is the relatively low cost of ITFS transmitting equipment compared to that of standard open-circuit broadcasting. However, while the 2500 MhZ signal is transmitted openly, the cost of special receiving antenna and converter exceeds the cost of normal home receiving equipment and, for practical purposes, only those institutions specifically utilizing the signals would likely make the investment. Maintenance is low in cost and does not require specially trained personnel."

ITFS has many advantages to recommend it, and the strong support of a number of satisfied users. There are, however, certain disadvantages:

1. The need to engage in local and regional cooperative planning for optimum use of available channels and for effective development of program resources.

2. Limitations on power and coverage area.

3. The need to obtain a license from the Federal Communications Commission.

4. The need for multiple studios and/or multiple dissemination sources such as video-tape recorders and film chains to serve a multichannel service.[10]

SATELLITE TRANSMISSION

In the 1960's, with the exception of a few isolated experiments, satellite transmission for instructional television was mostly theoretical. In the 1970's, it may perhaps play a more prominent part in the transmission of instructional television. As Wilbur Schramm noted, "The main difference between instructional television by satellite and instructional television without it is that the satellite will offer a much larger base of sharing resources, and a much quicker way of doing so. A new course, developed and produced by one of the national professional organizations—or by a university or school system —might be offered to all the nation's schools at once, if there were sufficient demand for it, rather than filtering slowly down through all the separate educational television outlets and individual school systems."[11]

Whatever method of transmission and distribution a school, school district, or state decides to utilize, it should plan the system with as much flexibility as possible. For instance, a school may decide that closed-circuit television will best serve its instructional purposes. In addition to needed facilities for closed-circuit television, the school planners would be wise to include antennas and distribution systems for the reception of broadcast signals as well. Technology has tended to outrun the educational system in the past, and a forward-looking administrator would render a valuable service to students, teachers, and parents by choosing the distribution and reception system that would allow maximum flexibility with a minimum of expense in remodeling, redesigning, or replacing outmoded equipment.

Television and Individualized Instruction

Although closed-circuit television and Instructional Television Fixed Service are more flexible than broadcast television, at times even more flexibility may be desired. As video-tape machines become smaller, lighter, and less expensive, there will be more and more possibilities for using them in the educational environment. Some day, perhaps, we shall see television and all of its associated equipment as a means of mediated instruction which may not be related to a means of distribution. For instance, broadcast television may be used in schools to present only those programs which are of national importance, live, from the scene of the event. This use would require a reevaluation of the entire concept of "broadcasting" as we now know it. It may mean a group of stations on a standby basis for transmission, or if the satellite does become available to education in the near future, it may simply mean that access to the satellite is guaranteed on a demand basis. Perhaps those stations which have played a prominent role in the production of instructional television materials will continue to do so, but they will not distribute the programs in the conventional manner. Program materials have already been distributed experimentally by means of a highly sophisticated information-retrieval system to video-tape recorders located in the schools in the area. Night transmission made all of the tapes available to the teacher the next day, and they could then be played on a portable video-tape recorder at his convenience.

A school, or some other type of learning environment, equipped with several video-tape recorders, video-playback units, and a reasonable supply of taped program material, could use the "mass medium" of television as an integral and prominent component in an individually prescribed learning program. In addition to taped materials from educational television stations, at least two commercial companies are offering taped materials in cartridge form which may be used with any standard television receiver equipped with a cartridge-playback unit.

Commercial firms, with astounding regularity, announce the promise or presence of yet another means of recording, playback, duplication, dial access, and the like, and always the technology is far out in front of our ability to accept or absorb it. Whatever the technology turns out to be, the philosophical, rational basis for use must precede its adoption. If the trend in education for the rest of the twentieth century is toward individually prescribed learning, we must be able to see television as one component in the instructional design, and we must be able to prescribe with some degree of accuracy and measurability just what we want television to do for the learner. There have been a great many glowing descriptions of the student at his study carrel with access to audio-tapes, television-tapes, cathode ray tube display devices, and the like, but until we have carefully thought out just exactly what it is that the student ought to be doing and learning on his own, with the "teacher-facilitator" to guide him, much of the crystal-ball gazing about the future of television in education will be nothing more than electronic rhetoric.

This view of the future of television may seem pessimistic, but individualized instruction, in general, has so far failed to make a real dent in the established patterns of education, and its future does not look promising unless we redefine the roles of the teacher, the student, and the administrator. Although it is certainly a moot proposition, I believe that individualized instruction is resisted because it goes against the pattern set for generations. Until we understand that resistance and devise strategies for coping with it, we are dealing only with the peripheral aspects of the problem.

Some Financial Considerations

Although many of the comments in the study made by the Fund for Media Research were favorable and enthusiastic, it was apparent that television's share of the total amount of instructional time was extremely small, and its share of the educational budget was a very small percentage of the total; in short, television's contribution to the educational systems of the sixteen cities studied was not very significant. There was much discussion of the problems of scheduling, quality of materials, and lack of coordination, but the problems beneath the surface were more compelling and more difficult to cope with. Obviously, there is insufficient financial support, and the arguments between school administrators and television administrators do nothing to help solve the problems. The school administrator frequently says that he would gladly lend more support to television if only the quality were better, and the television administrator replies that quality costs money, and the money is simply not available to do those things that would be imaginative, stimulating, and productive.

This argument does not lead anywhere, because the underlying premise is that television can very easily be included or not included in a learning environment, and its presence or absence is at best incidental to the process of learning. If this is the way it should be, could the same attitude be applied toward the use of textbooks—or teachers —or blackboards? Television has never been considered on the same level as the traditional elements in education, and the root of the financial problem is therefore as much a problem of educational philosophy as it is a question of educational economics.

One possible way to approach the financial problem of instructional television is to consider more carefully the economics of educational investment. An economist looking at the process of education would ask which of the many options, that is, buildings, personnel, media, and the like, would yield the greatest return on the investment, and plan a learning environment on that basis. A school administrator may find that the economist's point of view challenges all his notions about how to spend the educational dollar, but the time he spends on this economic analysis would be richly rewarding if the result is a greater yield on the investment, more efficiency in the school system, and ultimately a better human product.

The economic analysis might also lead to some rethinking about the rigidity of most educational budgets, which are usually organized in a traditional way. For this reason, it is difficult to accommodate any kind of innovative activity into the existing structure. The rigidity of the budget has frequently kept instructional television on the periphery of education, simply because the budget planners could not justify its use when faced with a budget reduction. Instructional television will not receive its share of the educational dollar until it is considered an integral part of the educational process, rather than an "extra" to be incorporated if the budget permits. It will then be budgeted according to the services it renders to each function of the learning institution. When it is considered as a part of science teaching, language teaching, or in-service education, the administrator will be able to justify its inclusion in his budget. The financing of instructional television thus seems dependent upon a reevaluation of the economic and educational worth of the options in education, which in turn may lead to a more flexible attitude toward overall budget planning for education.

Another factor to be considered is the pattern into which many educators have fallen of relying too heavily on external sources of funding, such as federal grant money or private foundation sources. Although the federal government through the Elementary and Secondary Education Act, the National Defense Education Act, and the ETV Facilities Act has been most generous in providing funds to start instructional television projects and to get them through the beginning stages, there is a danger in turning to government or foundation sources each time money is needed for instructional television. Administrators are relieved of having to make some very difficult decisions about how to spend their money, and television administrators are given a measure of security in their operations that would not exist if their products succeeded or failed according to the laws of supply and demand, economic competition, and value as determined in the market place. The federal government and the private foundations no doubt will continue to play a significant role in financing instructional television, but until educators see its integral part in the educational process, which can be analyzed philosophically and economically, it will remain an "extra" item in the budget, an unknown quantity as far as economic investment is concerned, and always subject to curtailment or elimination whenever educational funds are reduced.

Television in Instruction: An Appraisal was published by the Department of Audio-Visual Instruction of the National Education Association in the late 1950's. In the final section was a list of questions about the use of television to which answers must be found:

> 1. How may the television teacher and the classroom teacher communicate more effectively to increase the feedback from the learners?
>
> 2. How can televised instruction be adapted to the wide range of individual variation in capacity, interest, rate of learning, and readiness present in every class group?
>
> 3. What administrative planning patterns work best in operating a program of instructional television?
>
> 4. How can television help a student to evaluate his own learning?
>
> 5. How can television contribute to experimentation with the organization of the school—class size, grouping, arrangement of facilities, and time?
>
> 6. In what ways is television at its best as a medium of instruction? Are there significant differences depending upon age, subject matter, relations with other materials?
>
> 7. Can television make a unique contribution with respect to such societal problems as the shortage of skilled manpower, cultural tensions, and the need to locate and develop outstanding talent?
>
> 8. What can television do that cannot be accomplished as efficiently and effectively with other media?[12]

The pamphlet's concluding sentences were: "These are suggestive of the fields in which research and experimentation are needed in the immediate future. Only as they are examined can we assess with increasing accuracy the value that instructional television will ultimately have for American education." As we enter the decade of the seventies, it must be noted that definitive answers to many of these questions have not yet been made.

No one has all the answers to the future of television in education, and it may be hoped that there will never be a point at which everyone concerned can stop asking questions, experimenting and sometimes failing. We keep looking for new ideals and we keep falling short of them; we try new things and we frequently are discouraged and disappointed; but we are proud of those moments when television has helped to provide some truly meaningful learning experiences. Television has great potential in furthering the educational process, and we must continue to look for the best ways to help the learner to learn and the teacher to teach.

Selected Bibliography

SOME GENERAL REFERENCES

Allen, Dwight W., Richard J. Clark, and James Cooper. *Micro Teaching: A Description*. Stanford, California: Stanford Teacher Education Program, Stanford University, 1967.

Bosley, Howard E., and Harold E. Wigren. *Television and Related Media in Teacher Education, Some Exemplary Practices*. Baltimore, Maryland: Multi-State Teacher Education Project, 1967.

Chu, Goodwin C., and Wilbur Schramm. *Learning from Television: What the Research Says*. Stanford, California: The Institute for Communication Research, 1967.

Costello, Lawrence F., and George N. Gordon. *Teach with Television: A Guide to Instructional TV*. New York: Hastings House, 1961.

Diamond, Robert M., editor. *A Guide to Instructional Television*. New York: McGraw-Hill, 1964.

Educational Facilities Laboratories, Inc. *Design for ETV: Planning for Schools with Television*. Revised edition. New York: Educational Facilities Laboratories, Inc., 1968.

Griffith, Barton L., and Donald MacLennan, editors. *Improvement of Teaching by Television*. Columbia, Missouri: University of Missouri Press, 1964.

Koenig, Allen E., and Ruane B. Hill. *The Farther Vision: Educational Television Today*. Madison, Wisconsin: University of Wisconsin Press, 1969.

Lewis, Philip L. *Educational Television Guidebook*. New York: McGraw-Hill, 1961.

Murphy, Judith, and Ronald Gross. *Learning by Television*. New York: Fund for the Advancement of Education, 1966.

National Association of Educational Broadcasters, 1346 Connecticut Ave., Washington, D. C. 20036:
> *Bibliography of Educational Television and Related Communications Systems*, 1967.
> *Directory and Yearbook of Educational Broadcasting* (annual).
> *Educational Broadcasting Review* (bimonthly).
> *Fundamentals of Television Systems: A Technical Monograph for Non-Technical Personnel*, by W. J. Kessler, 1968.
> *NAEB Newsletter* (monthly).
> *Toward A Significant Difference*. Final Report of the National Project for the Improvement of Televised Instruction, 1968.

New Educational Media in Action: Case Studies for Planners, Parts I, II, III. UNESCO, International Institute for Educational Planning, 1969.

Pinney, Robert H., and Robert J. Miltz. *Television Recordings and Teacher Education: New Directions.* Stanford, California: Secondary Teacher Education Program, Stanford University, 1967.

Public Television, A Program for Action. Report of the Carnegie Commission on Educational Television. New York: Bantam Books, 1967.

Reid, J. Christopher, and Donald W. MacLennan. *Research in Instructional Television and Film.* Washington, D.C.: U.S. Government Printing Office, 1967.

Rossi, Peter H., and Bruce J. Biddle, editors. *The New Media and Education.* New York: Doubleday and Company, Inc., 1967.

Schramm, Wilbur, et al. *The New Media: Memo to Educational Planners.* UNESCO, International Institute for Educational Planning, 1967.

Schramm, Wilbur, editor. *The Impact of Educational Television.* Urbana, Illinois: University of Illinois Press, 1960.

Schramm, Wilbur, editor. *Educational Television: The Next Ten Years.* Stanford, California: The Institute for Communication Research, 1962. 2nd edition. Washington, D.C.: U.S. Government Printing Office, 1965.

Schueler, Herbert, and Gerald S. Lesser. *Teacher Education and the New Media.* Washington, D.C.: The American Association of Colleges for Teacher Education, National Education Association, 1967.

Smith, Mary H., editor. *Using Television in the Classroom.* New York: McGraw-Hill, 1961.

To Improve Learning. A Report to the President and the Congress of the United States by the Commission on Instructional Technology. Washington, D.C.: U.S. Government Printing Office, 1970.

Wigren, Harold E., Henry T. Ingle, and Michael Molenda. *A Survey of Instructional Closed-Circuit Television.* Washington, D.C.: Department of Audiovisual Instruction, National Education Association, 1967.

PERIODICALS

Audio-Visual Communications Review. Published quarterly by the Association for Educational Communications and Technology (formerly, Department of Audiovisual Instruction), National Education Association, Washington, D.C.

Audiovisual Instruction. Published monthly except July and August by AECT, Washington, D.C.

Educational/Instructional Broadcasting: The International Journal of Educational Radio and Television. Published monthly by Acolyte Publications, Los Angeles, California.

Educational Television International. Published quarterly by Pergamon Press Ltd., Oxford, England.

ETV Newsletter. Published biweekly by Tepfer Publishing Co., Ridgefield, Connecticut.

FILMS

For information on Films about Instructional Television write to:
NAEB TEACHING MATERIALS LIBRARY
Dr. Clair R. Tettemer
Northern Illinois University
Dekalb, Illinois 60115
See also "Films About Broadcasting," *Journal of Broadcasting,* XI, No. 3, 1966-67.

SOURCES OF INFORMATION AND ADVICE
ABOUT INSTRUCTIONAL TELEVISION

ERIC Clearinghouse on Educational Media and Technology
    Institute for Communication Research
    Stanford University
    Stanford, California 94305
Great Plains National Instructional Television Library
    University of Nebraska, Lincoln, Nebraska 68508
National Association of Educational Broadcasters
    1346 Connecticut Avenue N.W.
    Washington, D.C. 20036
National Education Association
    Division of Educational Technology
    1201 16th Street N. W.
    Washington, D.C. 20036
National Educational Television
    10 Columbus Circle
    New York, N.Y. 10019
National Instructional Television
    Box A
    Bloomington, Indiana 47401

Notes

INTRODUCTION

1. *Highlighting the Progress of American Education:* OE-100 (Washington, D.C.: U.S. Government Printing Office, 1967).

2. John I. Goodlad, "The Future of Learning and Teaching," at the inauguration of Sam M. Lambert as Executive Secretary, National Education Association, Washington, D.C., October 20, 1967.

CHAPTER 3

1. National Association of Educational Broadcasters, *1971 Directory and Yearbook of Educational Broadcasting* (Washington, D.C., 1971).

2. National Association of Secondary School Principals, *The Principalship* (Washington, D.C., 1965).

3. "How Parents Feel," *Time,* June 3, 1966, p.51.

4. Harold E. Wigren, "Creating Better Learning Opportunities on Instructional Television" (Washington, D.C.: NEA, January, 1966), p. 1.

5. Melvin W. Barnes, "More Time to Teach," *Atlantic Monthly,* 206 (November, 1960), 128.

6. Presley D. Holmes, *Educational Broadcasting Research* (Washington, D.C.: NAEB, 1964).

7. Wilbur Schramm, ed., *Educational Television: The Next Ten Years* (Stanford, Calif.: The Institute for Communication Research, 1962), p. 5.

8. Lee S. Dreyfus and Gary Gumpert, "Students Visit Via Satellite," *NAEB Journal,* 25 (May–June, 1966), 13.

9. "What Is a Well-Educated Man?" *NEA Journal,* LI (April, 1962), p. 22.

CHAPTER 7

1. Wilbur Schramm, "What We Know about Learning from Instructional Television," *Educational Television: The Next Ten Years* (Stanford, Calif.: The Institute for Communication Research, 1962), p. 64.

2. Charles J. McIntyre, "Applying Learning Theory to Televised Instruction." *NAEB Journal,* 24, No. 6 (November–December, 1965), 54-63.

3. I am emphasizing this point, because it is shown later that some research projects do not answer the questions that the researcher thinks he is asking. For instance, in a research project with some other label it is quite possible to ask unwittingly whether high-aptitude students learn more than low-aptitude students.

4. David W. Stickell, "A Critical Review of the Methodology and Results of Research Comparing Television and Face-to-Face Instruction" (Ed.D. thesis, The Pennsylvania State University, 1963).

5. The following sources are recommended for at least an initial exposure to such literature:

Audio-Visual Communication Review.

Educational Broadcasting Review.

Arthur A. Lumsdaine and Mark A. May, "Mass Communications and Educational Media," *Annual Review of Psychology,* 16 (1965), 475-534.

J. Christopher Reid and Donald W. MacLennan, *Research in Instructional Television and Film* (Washington, D.C.: U.S. Government Printing Office, 1967).

Goodwin C. Chu and Wilbur Schramm, *Learning from Television: What the Research Says* (Stanford, Calif.: The Institute for Communication Research, 1967).

CHAPTER 8

1. John I. Goodlad, "The Future of Learning and Teaching" at the inauguration of Sam M. Lambert as Executive Secretary, National Education Association, Washington, D.C., October 20, 1967.

2. John M. Culkin, S. J., "A Schoolman's Guide to Marshall McLuhan" *Saturday Review,* March 18, 1967, p.72.

3. *Public Television: A Program for Action* (Report of the Carnegie Commission on Educational Television. New York: Bantam Books, 1967), p. 81.

4. Judith Murphy and Ronald Gross, *Learning by Television* (New York: Fund for the Advancement of Education, 1966).

5. *Public Television: A Program for Action,* pp. 81-82.

6. C. R. Carpenter, Final Report, *Quality of Instructional Materials,* U.S. Office of Education Bureau of Research Contract: OEC-1-7-0771142-4372, The Pennsylvania State University, University Park, Pennsylvania, August, 1969, p. 29.

7. Edwin G. Cohen, NCSCT News, Volume 2, Number 1, 1967.

8. *School Television: Great Cities, 1967* (Chicago: Fund for Media Research, 1967), p. B-8.

9. Harold Wigren, "ETV: An Unfulfilled Promise?" A speech delivered at the American Association of School Administrators Convention, Atlantic City, N. J., February, 1966.

10. *Instructional Television Fixed Service (2500 megahertz): What It Is . . . How to Plan* (Washington, D.C.: National Education, 1967), pp. 16-17.

11. Wilbur Schramm, *Instructional Television: Promise and Opportunity* (Washington, D.C.: NAEB, Instructional Division, Monograph Service, Issue 4, 1967), p. 21.

12. *Television in Instruction: An Appraisal* (Washington, D.C.: Department of Audio-Visual Instruction, National Education Association, 1958), p. 24.

Index

Administration of educational TV: of a station, 53-55; of a closed-circuit system, 39-53; communication within school system, 6-7, 35, 123-24; and curriculum selection, 44-47; financial aspects, 94-95, 131-32; and lesson development, 89-91; and lesson utilization, 91-93; and telecast preparation, 50-51; programming, 43-44; responsibility for classroom use, 21; responsibility to the community, 87; responsibility to schools, 87-89; school administrator's role, 38-56; station administrator's role, 86-96; and team teaching, 44-47

Administrators: and communication within school system, 6-7, 35, 123-24; role in starting a school TV system, 38-56; role in directing a station, 86-96

Adult education, 124-25

"Adventures in Science," 15-17

Affective learning, 99-100

American Government TV course, 100, 105, 106-7, 109

Attitude toward TV: of classroom teacher, 26-28; of parents, 24; of principals, 23-24; of pupils, 15-17, 100, 105, 109

Auctions, on-the-air, 95

Barnes, Melvin, 30

Behavioral sciences: and TV recordings, 8

Bibich, George, 38

Bloomington, Ind., 27, 119

Blue Ridge ETV Association, Inc., 87, 88, 92, 95

Boston, Mass., 94, 95

Broadcast TV, 53-55, 125-26

Budgeting for TV, 131-32

Burke, Richard, 114

Carnegie Commission: study of public TV, 17-19, 117-18

Carpenter, C. R., quoted, 118-19

Characteristics: of TV, 3-9; of a good TV teacher, 58-62

Charles F. Kettering Foundation, 24

Chicago, Ill., 41, 62, 95; junior college TV experiment, 26, 32

Child, Julia, 94

Cinko, Louis, 54

Classroom teacher: and advance information on telecasts, 82-84; attitudes toward TV, 26-28; team role with TV teacher, 11-13, 28, 29-30, 61-62, 82-84; and utilization of TV lesson, 27, 28, 32-33, 91-92

Classroom use of TV, 10-22; administrator's role in, 21; advantages of, 17-19; roles of classroom and TV teacher, 11-13, 61-62; criticisms of, 19-20; physical arrangements for, 20-21, problems with, 14; pupil reaction to, 15-17, 30, 31; telecast procedure for, 13-14

Cleveland, Ohio, 91

Closed-circuit systems: administration of, 39-53; advantages of, 126-27

Cohen, Edwin G., quoted, 119-20

Color TV, 20, 54

Columbus, Ohio, 64, 65

Communication model, 102-3, 109

Consortium productions, 120

Cooperation between classroom and TV teachers, 11-13, 61-62

Cost of TV equipment, 42

Counseling programs, 34-35, 49-52

Cox, E. Dana, 86

"Crawls," 72

Cues for TV teacher, 79

Culkin, John, quoted, 116

Curriculum: committees for TV, 88; coordinating TV programs with, 21; enrichment, 115-16; and high school use of TV, 25-26; selection for TV, 44-47

Director of TV series: role of, 89-92; and TV teacher, 62-63

ning for, 118-20; preschool use, 125; presentations on, 5-6; quality of, 117-18; questions about, 114-33; responsibility of, 8-9; satellite transmission of, 128-29; in secondary schools, 23-37; stations, 125-26; teacher on, 57-85; teacher education by, 121-24; transmission of, 125-29; 2500 MhZ system, 127-28; as a visual medium, 121

Instructional Television Fixed Service (ITFS), 127-28

International Seminar on Instructional Television, 61

ITV. *See* Instructional television

Jacksonville, Fla., 95
Julius Caesar, 28

Kettering Foundation, 24
Kirksville, Mo., Public School System, 21
KQED, 68, 95

Lake Central High School, Dyer, Ind., 38, 53
Lake Central School Corporation, Ind., 38-56
Lake County, Ind., 53, 54
Lasswell, Harold, 102-3, 109
Learning: affective, 99-100; research on, 31, 97-113; from TV, evaluated, 97-113
Lerner, Max, 33
Lesson on TV: development of, 89-91; planning and execution of, 68-82; utilization of, 91-93
Libraries of taped lessons, 32
Licensing: ETV, 54; ITFS, 127-28
Lighting, TV, 72
Lunch-period scheduling, 94

Machiavelli, Niccolò, quoted, 10
Madison, Wis., 36
Major resource TV series, 64-65
Manuals for classroom teachers, 82-84
McIntyre, Charles, quoted, 101
Measurement problems of TV research, 100-1
Media differences and ITV research, 103-8
Memory aids for TV teacher, 78-79
Methodology in TV research, 108-11
Micro-teaching, 7-8, 122
Midwest Program on Airborne Television Instruction (MPATI), 41
Mielke, Keith W., 97

Mitchell, Wanda B., 23
Monitors, studio TV, 82
Moriarity, Don, 40
"Mr. Rogers' Neighborhood," 125
Murphy, Judith, quoted, 117

National Association of Educational Broadcasters (NAEB), 23, 27
National Association of Secondary School Principals, 23-24
National Defense Education Act, 132; Title III, 41; Title VII, 112
National Education Association (NEA), 26-27; DAVI, 133
National Instructional Television Center (NIT), 27, 32, 119-20
New York, N.Y., 35
Non-classroom use of TV, 34-36

Ooghe, A. Edward, 15, 17
"Operation Alphabet," 64

Parents and TV, 24
Paris, France, 36
Performance techniques for TV teacher, 79-82
Personality of TV teacher, 62
Physical education TV series, 64-65
Planning for TV, 118-20
Portland, Ore., 30
Practice teachers. *See* Student teachers
Preparation of a telecast, 50-51
Preschool education, 125
Presentation, TV, 5-6, 29-30
Pre-service training, 30-31
Principals and TV, 23-24
Producer-director: role of, 89-92; and TV teacher, 62-63
Productions, consortium, 120
Program underwriting, 94
Programming for TV, 43-44
Programs: American Government, 100, 105-6, 109; health-science, 65-67; homeroom, 47-50; physical education, 64-65
Purdue University, 61

Qualifications of a good TV teacher, 59-62
Quality of televised instruction, 117-18

Reading problems and TV, 121
"Rear controls" placement, 20-21
Receivers, closed-circuit TV, 42
Recorders: for individualized instruction, 129-30; for instant replay, 7; for playback of TV lesson, 24